Born in Montreal, Don graduated from the Montreal Graphic Arts Technical Foundation in 1979 and decided to move to Nova Scotia that same year. With letter writing being the primary means of communicating with family and friends, Don began writing stories of the farming experiences he encountered. Always the storyteller, Don honed his given ability for a formal presentation of his stories.

I dedicate this book to the memory of my wife, Katy, and my friends who departed this world before me. To the men and women who shaped the world where I grew up in Terrebonne Heights and to friends who wanted these stories recorded before I took them to the grave.

Don Moore

Memories of "A Kid from the Heights"

AUSTIN MACAULEY PUBLISHERS™
LONDON * CAMBRIDGE * NEW YORK * SHARJAH

Copyright © Don Moore 2023

All rights reserved. No part of this publication may be reproduced, distributed, or transmitted in any form or by any means, including photocopying, recording, or other electronic or mechanical methods, without the prior written permission of the publisher, except in the case of brief quotations embodied in critical reviews and certain other non-commercial uses permitted by copyright law. For permission requests, write to the publisher.

Any person who commits any unauthorized act in relation to this publication may be liable to criminal prosecution and civil claims for damages.

All of the events in this memoir are true to the best of the author's memory. The views expressed in this memoir are solely those of the author.

Ordering Information
Quantity sales: Special discounts are available on quantity purchases by corporations, associations, and others. For details, contact the publisher at the address below.

Publisher's Cataloging-in-Publication data
Moore, Don
Memories of "A Kid from the Heights"

ISBN 9798886933604 (Paperback)
ISBN 9798886933611 (ePub e-book)

Library of Congress Control Number: 2023910895

www.austinmacauley.com/us

First Published 2023
Austin Macauley Publishers LLC
40 Wall Street, 33rd Floor, Suite 3302
New York, NY 10005
USA

mail-usa@austinmacauley.com
+1 (646) 5125767

This manuscript would have never reached publication if it wasn't for the encouragement and guidance of Dr. Zalman Amit, Diane Wheeler and Doug Cooke. Acknowledging them is easy, but thanking them would require another lifetime.

Table of Contents

Preface	11
The Pine Tree	13
Lucy	14
The Beaches	20
End of an Era	25
Cream Soda	28
Joe the Barber	32
Door to Door Delivery	35
1949, The Great Fire	39
Changing of the Signs	43
The Early Years	50
Stormy and Things Around the Kitchen	57
The Beer License	64
The Vermettes	66
1957	71
Dr. Paquin	77
St. Margaret's Sunday School	80
Lewis King School	85
Mrs. Cheney	91

Mr. Partridge	94
Soap Box Derby Incident	98
Younger Years with Dickie	104
La Boulangerie	107
Friday Night Movies	110
The Telephone	113
Christmas	117
The Corn Boil	122
Halloween Through the Years	125
Robinson's Farm	128
Terrebonne Heights "Field Day"	130
Rusty's	135
The Motorcycle Incident at Rusty's Restaurant	141
Yvon	144
Old Eddy Ellis	147
Mr. Thorne's Light Bulb	151
Nick Debruin	156
Terrebonne Bridge	159
The Bowling Alley	162
The Figaro	165
My Dad	169
Epilogue	172

Preface

Although this book contains stories about one specific village in Canada, shortly after the Second World War, thousands of similar small towns experienced the same developmental struggles throughout Canada. Terrebonne Heights was one such village, located 25 miles north of Montreal, across the Rivière des Mille Îles, in the province of Québec.

While still a very young country itself, Canada, at this time, was also attempting to create its own worldly identity. Canada still did not have its own National Flag, nor had Scholars yet written our Constitution. Although 'Oh, Canada' was composed in 1880, then only to be acclaimed as Canada's National Anthem in 1990.

Perhaps, it could be as simple as exchanging the name of this village and its characters for the ones you experienced. Letting these pages and their stories transport you to a time and place that was so well spent for me.

And, if you had not yet been born, during this period in the 50s and 60s. These stories may give you some insight into this time in rural Canada. Each decade produces its generations, and this book is simply about the one I experienced.

This book refers to a factual village, actual experiences, and most importantly, it contains real people. I'm finding that it truly is only the people that matter. That creates those memories that keep returning us to our innocence and naivety, of days long since passed.

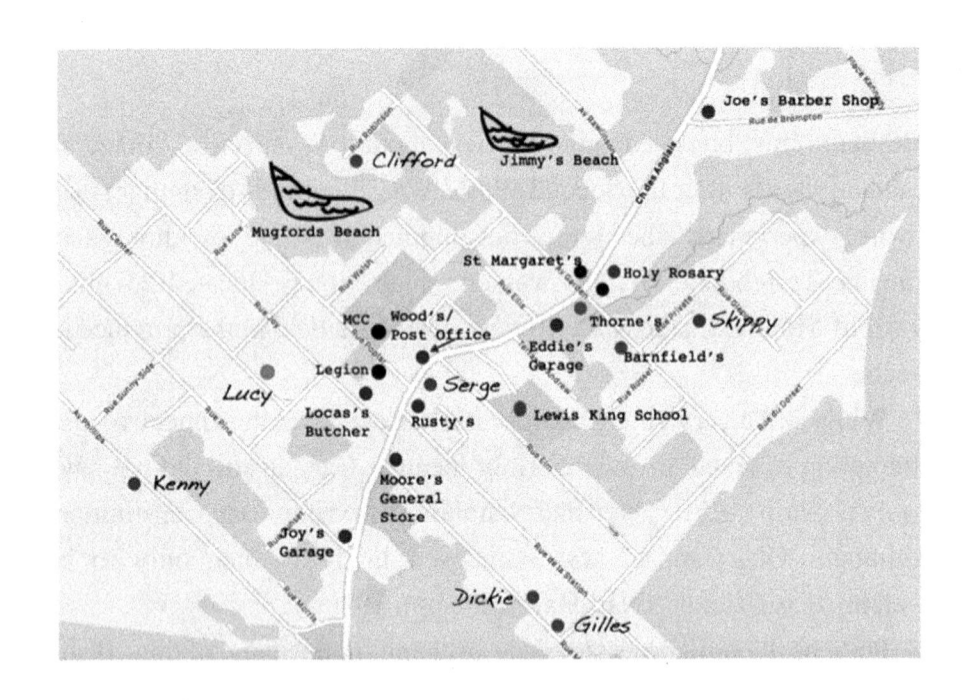

Terrebonne Heights, 1950

The Pine Tree

There was a huge pine tree near the corner of English and Station Roads before any development in that area. This Pine was 'our' tree. Serge Lévesque and I would go to Wood's store and buy a 5-cent big bottle of Kik Cola.

Then the largest bag of chips from my parents' store (Moore's General Store) lay around that old pine tree all day, plotting the upcoming course of our respective lives. We started and completed so many adventures under that old tree.

One could sense the relief of that old tree, as it seemed to sigh when it saw us coming with our supply of "food for thought" for another day travelling via daydreams.

We travelled the world, near and far, under that old tree. We left our youth behind under that old pine tree.

I miss my friend Serge and that old pine tree. Travelling was so much more fun with my friend Serge and that big old pine tree.

Lucy

With WW-II ending in 1945, tens of thousands of men and women arrived back in Canada, continuing to their respective home provinces to reunite with their families or begin life afresh, starting their own families.

My memory started in 1950, when I was about four years old with my family still living at my grandparent's home in Montréal at 543 Madeleine St., in Pointe-Saint-Charles, with my mom, dad, and younger sister Margaret Ann. When I was born, my dad had just received his honorable discharge after serving ten years of active duty in the Royal Canadian Navy. So, yes, more often than not, I was dressed in a sailor's outfit, and my grandfather always called me his little "Skipper." Over the years, most of my aunts and uncles lost any memory of my given name, and I became Skipper. Shortened to Skip over the years, a shield I wore proudly for decades.

My parents also had a summer cottage on Center Road in Terrebonne Heights. What an incredible stroke of good fortune this would turn out to be for me, at this time in my young life, and for my entire life journey.

During the week, my dad worked at the Canadian Naval Supply Depot in Montréal. He would come up to the Heights on the weekends. The trip from Montréal was a long, mostly wandering one. Once Dad crossed over the Pie-IX bridge off the island of Montréal, he would continue driving north, arriving at the village of Laval. The remaining road network to Terrebonne would slowly lead from village to town, eventually arriving at the Terrebonne Bridge.

Terrebonne was a beautiful village full of unique Québécois-style homes. These early constructions were usually rectangular structures of one-story, evolving into two-story building structures. These buildings were designed with an extremely tall and steep roof, sometimes almost twice as tall as the house below, to help prevent snow accumulation. These '18th' century houses were usually built of wood, although the surviving ones in Terrebonne mainly were constructed of fieldstone.

It was a long trip for my dad, but every time, I would be sitting on the front steps, waiting for my dad to arrive. It was always pure joy for us when Dad came to our cottage.

Meanwhile, my mom would have some older cousins stay with us for the summer months. Because neither Margaret Ann nor I were in school, Mom and the kids would venture to the Heights in June and stay too late in September. Even at this young age, I felt that there was something magical about this summer cottage on Center Road. I loved every morning, sunshine or rain; it didn't seem to matter. This place was that distinct.

Later in life, I wished we had named our cottage; it deserved a name. I would have named her "Lucy." Meaning "Born at Dawn," as this is where this Don's journey began.

Our little Lucy had an icebox on the front stoop; an old hand pump supplied cold, clean water, a small wood stove to take the chill off when necessary, and electric lighting. There was an outhouse out back; I can't remember if it was a one or a two-seater, but I remember how cold it could be.

I also remember how we'd scoot across those cold floors on those cool mornings to the safety of the warm sofa waiting to embrace us. Mom would make us "egg-in-a-glass"—pieces of chopped-up buttered toast with a soft-boiled egg stirred in. If you haven't eaten toast made on an old wood stove, you just haven't eaten toast yet.

Other than Mom taking a bottle of Mercurochrome, unscrewing the cap with that little glass rod attached, and dabbing Mercurochrome on the issue of the moment. Injuries could have been anything, from a cut knee to a limb's near amputation—Mercurochrome was to the rescue. Then, Mom treated a cut knee, a sneeze, and a wasp sting with an "Egg-in-a-glass." Yes, there was magic in an "egg-in-a-glass."

Now having a bath was always a significant production. Having to heat the water on the stove and fill up the tub, okay, never was that old steel tub ever full, but there would be enough water to get wet and wash.

Drinking water in the Heights was plentiful and relatively easy to access. Sand made up the entire Heights area, and you would be hard-pressed to find anything resembling a stone, let alone a boulder. The two standard methods to access water were digging a well or driving a 'point' into the ground until you hit a water seam. The point was a spear-shaped filter attached to the bottom of the pipe, a prevalent method for a cottage.

A residence would often opt for a dug well, with neighbors helping neighbors, facilitating the process, and safety concerns related to this project. Once the initial hole started, a three-foot-high by four-foot diameter cement well casing would be lowered into the cavity. The digging would continue with an additional culvert added as needed. Usually, one man in the well and another at the surface would raise the bucket and empty it before lowering it back into the well. The final stage would be to cap the well.

It is now 1951; I was five years old, so I would always be dirty enough to be the last one in the tub.

Mom: "Come on, Skipper, you're next."

Me: "But Mom, I'm only half dirty tonight."

Mom: "And I don't want to know which half young man, so we're going to wash all of you tonight."

Me: "Mom, I'll really try to get all dirty tomorrow, so we're not wasting water washing clean places, okay."

By then, the water was neither clean nor warm, but a comforting fluffy towel was always waiting for me.

There were chores to be done by my older cousins in the mornings. At the same time, I was looking for frogs or chasing the chickens. Then, it was off to the beach for the day, with a picnic.

We'd walk along Center Road toward Sunny Side Road because the other option, Park Row Road, only extended from Pine Road to Joy Road. Sunny Side was more of a laneway than a road, but it did cross over Joy Road to Poplar Road, leading to the entrance to Mugford's beach. One of two beaches in the Heights.

The two beaches established the first 'zones' in the Heights. The entrance to Jimmy's beach was off Garden Road. Garden Road intersected with English Road; it ran north and south. It also physically divided the village in half. So, anyone living east of Garden Road would often go to Jimmy's, and those living west of Garden Road tended to go to Mugford's.

Sometimes, on the way to the beach, a dust devil would form on one of those scorching hot days, and the wildflowers would be swirling around while the blowing sands whirled up from the road. I'd close my eyes as quickly as possible, but they liked to watch the flowers. So I usually ended up getting sand in my eyes. But Mom would always be there for me.

Mom: "Skipper, I told you to close your eyes when this happens."

Me: "I told them to close, Mom, but they wanted to look at the flowers."

Mom: "At the flowers, eh…Oh Lord, give me strength."

Mugford's had this white sugary color sand that would be warm and inviting. Now, I had red hair and freckles. Yes, the Irish in me, subjecting me to be very prone to getting sunburnt.

Even so, my mom would coat me with baby oil to protect me back in the day. Her intentions were wholesome; however, the results were inevitable, with me repeatedly getting burnt. These red welts would soon become blisters. With my skin being so sensitive, the thought of someone touching me would cause me pain.

Then, the Milk of Magnesia would be applied, drying to a flaky thin plaster-like substance. Which honestly seemed to help my mother more than it ever helped me. And 'aloe vera' at this time was still someone saying hello to someone named Vera. This constant burning would lead to severe issues for me later in life. But, at the time, life was fantastic. A white t-shirt solved most of these issues, protecting me in and out of the water.

My older cousins, May and Alan, spent summers with us from 1947 until 1954, when my parents bought their store. May was eleven years older than me, and Alan was nine years older.

Alan was constantly tormenting us with snakes of any variety he could find. Even being told that these snakes were harmless and couldn't hurt me, I was not convinced. Alan was always eager to confirm that he knew of people, who died from snakebites and some, that only had a few fingers fall off due to the snake's poison. He would tie snakes to the fence and chase me with them, and the worst was when he tied them to the gate, where he knew I had to pass.

Consequently, for the remainder of my life and even today, I have this apprehension, this anxiety or fear that something wrong or unpleasant will happen involving a snake. I'm sure he only saw it as fun while teasing his vulnerable young cousin; it wasn't.

On the other hand, May was so much fun to be around. She tended to spoil her cute little redheaded cousin and adored my blond, blue-eyed little sister Margaret Ann.

I'm sure my dad appreciated May staying at "Lucy" all summer. Her Venus attractiveness allured many a young man to visit, culminating with them picking up that giant old scythe and helping Dad with the chore of cutting the deep grasses around our cottage. My mom enjoyed May's company, too, as they were birds of a feather in their beauty and joie de vivre nature.

Each spring, Dad would order his baby chicks from the hatchery, arriving in crates at the train station in Terrebonne. Knowing how much I loved the sight and sounds of those big steam engines, Dad ensured that we would always arrive early, allowing me to be there for the train's arrival. Standing on the platform, I'd hear the train's whistle as it reached the Terrebonne train bridge. This enormous eruption of steam cascading the station would mark its arrival.

Once Dad stowed the chicks in the truck, he would wait so I could watch the train pull out of the station. The engine's wheels would make one rotation with a big grunt, with the train standing motionless. The clunking of the cars taking up the slack would soon echo down the train's length. The train slowly crept forward with each additional straining rotation, shortly departing the station.

A blast from the old train whistle signaled its final farewell. I fell asleep on the trip home, transporting me aboard the engine's cab, with my hand on the throttle and a smile on my face.

With the sun now setting, yet hiding behind the towering Pine trees, while bringing on nightfall, ending another day in the Heights, the stars would begin their appearance. And although we didn't have a vast night sky, because of the enclosing Pines, these open, blackened areas would become filled with millions of stars, a brilliance unimpeded by city lights and the like.

The heat of the day would surrender to the cooling night air, a freshness many today will never experience. I'm now in bed as my mom tucks me in, telling me she loves me.

The Beaches

As the sunlight poked into my bedroom, I anticipated heading to the beach again sometime today. My only job was staying out of trouble while Mom and May cleaned up the house. This staying out of trouble was never easy for me and not as easy as it sounded. The problem with staying out of trouble when you're young is that you don't know it's trouble until you're in it.

I peeked out to see what my cousin Allan might be scheming. Allan was fun when he wasn't tormenting me with snakes he had befriended. I could see Margaret Ann heading to the kitchen, already in her bathing suit and carrying her pail. A sure sign that soon, we'd be off to Mugford's.

Mugford's was the first beach I remembered going to, as it was the closest to our summer cottage on Center Road. As my mom prepared the picnic basket and got our towels and blankets ready for our day at the beach, I would be anxiously waiting on Lucy's front stoop with my younger sister Margaret Ann.

The sun had been up for a few hours, and all the dew had disappeared from the spider's webs, making the traps disappear. I always liked it when the crickets were chirping in the morning, as it was usually a sign of a good day. I loved the crickets at night too, but I think I may have been alone with that one.

As we walked along Sunny Side, my cousin Allan led the way, as usual. Margaret Ann was with Mom and May, following closely behind Allan. At the same time, I'm trailing behind, with my stick clicking along the white picket fences, while still trying to pick berries. Mom soon had me walking in front of her.

Only the primary roads had gravel in the Heights, leaving the remaining sand roads. These sand roads were worn by the cars continuously travelling along the same area of these narrow country roads, creating a grassy area between the tracks and along the borders of these roads. With trees lining most streets; Red Maple, Sugar Maple, White Birch, gracious Elms, and lots of Pine trees, renowned by the Heights residents. These trees formed an umbrella of shade along these old country roads. They concluded with this short walk to Mugford's, being a pleasant one.

As the seasons changed along the walk to and from the beach, the berry picking did too. From the raspberry season to my favorite, strawberry season, to BlackBerry season. Although seemingly plentiful enough along the side of the roads, there were fields of strawberries scattered throughout the Heights. Mom also had a few special patches for gathering Blackberries during their whole season. Mom's BlackBerry jam was my favorite of them all.

As soon as I saw the entrance to the beach, I would run ahead, trying to catch up to Allan. The access to the beach was a tree-lined sand road leading to a parking area in amongst the Pine trees. Adjacent to this open wooded space next to the canteen, someone would usually be checking for your pass. Or would be collecting a dime for a single person or a quarter for a family stay. Mom always bought the Family Season Pass.

There were changing rooms and an outhouse as well, near the canteen. Sometimes, the door latch to the changing room was out of reach. I would crawl under one of the walls rather than try and open the door latch. Often to the screams of someone already getting changed in there.

The walk to the water was a gentle sandy slope down to the dam. Then once crossed, opening up to a larger sandy beach area, usually filled with kids making sandcastles. The surface coverage with the white sugary sands in the Heights. Parents and adults appreciated how gentle the slope leading to the water area was. A similar downslope continued into the water, letting us kids get to the water while pushing and shoving each other, trying to be the first one.

A twelve-foot straight drop with a walkway ran parallel to the water below the canteen. Railway ties shored up this walkway, creating a retaining wall of sorts. The older boys would run and scream, jumping off this upper area, leaping and clearing the six feet needed to miss the retaining wall and safely enter the water.

I couldn't wait to be old enough "to run like a young Comanche Brave, leaping off this high mountain cliff, to save a young Indian Maiden in distress, trapped in the threatening waters below." Mom usually laughed, saying that I had an over-active imagination. One for which she loved me.

On any cloudless blue sky day, the beach's sun worshipers, beachgoers, and people have fun splashing as laughter fills the air. Mugford's, too, it seemed, was a unique place where memories began. A place where time stood still. Families gathered to share the day lazily, laid back, a place where time didn't seem to exist. You came whenever you came, and you left whenever you left. Mugford's "the sands of time."

There were two small streams located in the Heights. One ran on the south side of English Road, traversing through the populated area of the Heights. At the same time, the second started north of where Joy Road ended, flowing west toward Brompton Road, where these streams would merge, continuing to pour into Lac Henri in Mascouche, Victorice's beach. These waters were the bases for all three beaches in the area.

Mr. Mugford used whatever means were available at the time to create a dam that lasted years. The wooden wall also lessened the risk of erosion along the Westside.

The next beach created along this watercourse was Mr. Robinson's "Jimmy's Beach." Both were very similar in size and design. The water and beach areas at Jimmy's may have been slightly smaller, but the beachgoers equally loved both. Jimmy's canteen had a more sizeable dance hall and a steeper embankment opposite the beachside. Jimmy's also had a diving board.

The depth of water in both would be about five feet at most. Similarly, it was a dime for one day's stay at the beach and twenty-five cents for a family. "Jimmy's" also offered a Family Pass. There was more of a treed area at Jimmy's, providing more shade for picnics, or some of us, to escape the sun's rays and the day's heat.

We'd spend hours playing in the water at either beach with Robyn, Gail, Katy, Chrissie, Rosemary, Kathy and my sister, among others. At the same time, splashing and dunking the girls, or carrying them on our shoulders, while the girls would try to push each other over. We chased them around the beach with our towels, making the towels snap. As Rock and Roll ruled the day, someone always had a portable radio. So many young crushed hearts, sharing these summer days idled away at the beach. I would later come to appreciate it as days well spent, very well spent.

It wasn't unusual to find a family with passes to both of these beaches, with them only a short distance apart with groups spending time at one beach, then heading to the other to meet more friends and spend the remainder of the day with them. During the 1950s, it was common practice that the parks and beaches would be closed at sunset. These two beaches in the Heights also closed for the day at sunset.

The third beach in the area did not come into play in the Heights until the late 50s or early 60s. There was also a small lake where these two streams merged and ended in Lac Henri, known locally as Victorice's Beach, located on the outskirts of Ville de Mascouche.

This beach was much more than a simple, artificial country beach. The water area itself was the size of a tiny lake. It also had more facilities, including three rafts, a diving board, and a three-level diving tower.

When we were twelve, we would go with our bikes along English Road, travelling to Robinson's Farm. An old cow trail running through their woodland led directly to a grazing area, but more importantly, to the beach. This shortcut through Robinson's farm kept us safely out of harm's way.

My sister and her friends also mentioned this sense of well-being, of being in safe hands. Just a very comforting experience; what a uniquely special time and place to be a kid from the Heights.

End of an Era

The Heights was such a fun place to grow up in the 50s and 60s, and Mugford's beach was one of those memorable places. Word had it that old man Mugford built his dam from everything available to him at the time. From old mattresses and wooden wagon wheels to virtually anything that would trap the sands and start to dam up the waterway. Eventually, he managed to block the stream running through a part of his property.

Through his efforts, a recreational beach was established, providing a much-needed outlet for the people living in Terrebonne Heights to enjoy swimming in this area. This dam lasted for years until the Mascouche Community Club took it over. I don't know if they purchased the property or assumed the responsibility of maintaining the dam.

In either case, it did not work out for the betterment of the community, and in fact, it turned into an enormous disaster.

After years of continual service of Mugford's dam, the MCC decided to remove and replace this old self-made dam with a newer engineer-designed cement dam. One that would have an adjustable flume providing for better water height regulation.

Dickie, Serge, Gilles, and I, went down to watch the construction of the new dam, anticipating that the surface area of the water, once frozen this winter, would give us a terrific place to play hockey. We watched in amazement as these huge bulldozers and excavators readily removed the debris from the old dam while preparing the site for the new concrete one.

I told Dickie that I wanted to be a bulldozer operator when I grew up. He just laughed, "Until tomorrow, eh Skip."

Unfortunately, even before the water could freeze, there were signs of erosion at the dam's base. By the spring, the water had created a watercourse under the new dam. A second dam was designed and installed with much the same results.

The Partridge's homestead abutted up against Mugford's, and Clifford saw me looking at the engineering results.

Clifford: "So, what do you think Moore?"

Me: "I think we'll be skating on the small frozen creek area again this winter."

Clifford: "They should have left matters alone, Old man Mugford knew how to dam up the water."

Me: "Better than a Beaver, I'd say."

My only other memory from this period was one fit for a movie scene. We were all too young to see this happen, but the story that went around was.

That very late one night, young Eddy and Earl decided to take one of the Provincial buses to Mugford's, where they drove it across the dam. Now, this might not sound like an impressive feat, but when you consider that these boys weren't exactly sober and that the dam width was six inches less than the wheelbase of the bus, it starts to become quite impressive.

However, it was not impressive to the bus company, as none of their drivers would attempt to drive the bus back across the dam. The negotiated outcome was all charges would be dropped if young Eddy would bring the bus back across the dam successfully, that is. Eddy managed to return the bus to the owners unscathed, but the dam would shortly start to disintegrate.

We never did get another chance to swim at Mugford's, but once that creek had frozen over, we could usually all be found there during the daylight hours playing hockey. And on any moonlight night, more often than not, some girls would join us skating there too. As for where people skated, if it had an ice surface, you'd probably find someone skating on it.

The hockey rink never had any outdoor lighting to allow us to play hockey at night. So, some nights there would be a skating party where it seemed that everyone would show up. Usually, at the start of the evening, people would start skating around, enjoying each other's company. Then, with one of the boys being the anchor, we all held hands, forming a line to create a "whip." People toward the end of this line would soon be whipping around until either the person at the very end of the line, or a few people near the end, would be unable to maintain their balance, and the laughter would begin. It was such a great, carefree, fun time.

The 'dam' episode ended Mugford's, a beach that had made so many memories for years. A beach that was more like an old friend than simply being sand and water. I grew up on the sands at Mugford's, not realizing that things were starting to change when Mugford's closed slowly. And you know, I'd say that ignorance, in this case, was bliss.

They say that you cannot go back. Well, I don't have to go back; I was there when it mattered.

Cream Soda

In the spring of 1953, my parents negotiated to secure funding to purchase Hart's General Store. With this endeavor, they sold their cottage on Center Road, our little "Lucy," while raising the required capital for this transaction.

During this period, they rented a home on Maple Road near the store. My parents were being groomed and tutored by Mr. and Mrs. Hart. Along with learning the business aspects of the store, it would be the continuation of Hart's rapport with its customers that would lead to its ongoing success.

I liked it when our parents brought Margaret Ann and me to the store. Mrs. Hart adored my little sister and always had a small brown bag of penny candies waiting for the both of us. My mom seemed to acquire this penny candy technique successfully from Mrs. Hart.

The winter temperatures in the Heights would go from moderate to a depth that even the Devil would have trouble tolerating, all in a matter of minutes. December 31st, 1953, was one of those bone-chilling nights, with the mercury dipping to minus thirty.

Looking out the window of our home on Maple Road, I watched my breath frost up the glass. I was pressing my nose against the glass, waiting for our cousins Dorothy and Lillian to come to babysit Margaret Ann and me tonight.

Mom and Dad would be attending the annual New Year's Eve dance at the Mascouche Community Club. The hall could easily accommodate two hundred people. Ceiling support posts decorated with a big red bow and streamers would be draped from post to post. The highlight of the evening would be the cascading balloons at midnight.

This dance was always 'The' event of the year. Couples would be decked out in their finest while joining their friends and neighbors in a night of live music and a good old time.

The Royal Canadian Legion, Branch 120, also held their dance on New Year's Eve. The community could easily support both of these organizations in the Heights. There was no doubt that once these dances had ended in the morning, many of those old cars would be unwilling to start. Turning the keys would surely result in a chorus of moaning and groaning. Old Eddy's Garage services would be busy tonight and well into the morning, trying to jump-start those old girls.

Margaret Ann and I were excited, as our older cousins Dorothy and Lillian would mind us tonight. Mom had left chips, some peanuts, and baked treats. Mom bought the baked treats, as her baking reputation was well known. This past summer, Mom made jam tarts for my friends and me for my birthday party. She was so pleased that all the kids kept coming back for more. She said to Dorothy, "Look at that, they love my jam tarts, and they all keep coming back wanting more."

Dorothy, either didn't have the heart or maybe, it was the nerve to tell Mom that they weren't eating the tarts; they just wanted them refilled with more jam.

So, finally, Mom and Dad left for the dance. It didn't sound like Dad's old Dodge was ever going to start for a while. With a few more spurts and wheezes, a small bang and the old girl started purring. Life was good.

There was no TV back then, so the radio supplied the entertainment with music, and live commentary of events, in and around, Montréal. Dorothy and Lillian played games with us and chased us around the house. We even had a pillow fight.

We were in our pajamas and had slippers on because the floor was freezing. The old house would make this intense snap once in a while as the temperature continued to plummet. You could feel that deep coldness creeping through those draughty old walls. Frost had long since covered the windows, and the curtains danced, escorted by the cold air leaking through the cracked windowpane.

Dorothy put out the chips and treats while Lillian poured the drinks. I couldn't wait as Mom had bought Cream Soda for the first time. Usually, Mom would always buy Cokes. I looked at those white bubbles of Cream Soda dancing in my glass, and when I took a sip. It felt like my eyes would pop out of my head and dance around the room; it was that good. I could stay up all night drinking this Cream Soda. But Lillian had other ideas. One more small glass, and then you're off to bed.

"No, no, no," I wanted to stay up longer.

So now I'm in bed. Margaret Ann fell asleep on Dorothy's lap and was also in her bed. I can hear them laughing and having a good time. Sticking my head out of my bedroom door, I begged for just one more tiny drink of Cream Soda. Please, even smaller than tiny, please. The answer wasn't a good one. Get back in bed, young man and go to sleep. Go to sleep with all that Cream Soda out there. There must be a way; there has to be a way. That's it.

I'm seven years old, and I'm out of there. I bolted for the front door in my pajamas and bare feet.

"Oh s-h-i-t, no, no, no, come back, Skipper…"

I'm out the door and under the front steps. With their boots and winter coats on, Dorothy and Lillian were now outside with a flashlight, calling for me.

Lillian screamed, "Skipper, get back here, or you'll be in trouble."

I could hear Dorothy say, "And you think that will bring him back inside."

Then it happened, Dorothy saying, "If you come inside, you'll get more Cream Soda."

By this time, my teeth were chattering, like Grandma's teeth, submerged in that old water glass sitting on her night table when the train went by. They wrapped me in some big blankets and continued rubbing my feet with their warm hands. Lillian gave me a drink of

Cream Soda, and soon, I was getting warm. My teeth started to chatter again, and Dorothy told Lillian to pour me a little more Cream Soda.

Wait a minute, if my teeth chatter, I get more Cream Soda. So I tried to make my teeth chatter. And chatter they did. "Look, he's shivering and chattering." Lillian poured another glass of Cream Soda. With the suggestion of going to bed, my teeth seemed to chatter again. This scenario would be a New Year's Eve to remember.

The next room I'm in, is the bathroom, or more to the point, the toilet. Only being seven and now dying, there wasn't much to pass before my eyes ahead of me dying.

Will I ever see my mom again? Who's going to feed "Betty," my Goldfish?

This experience would be the first time I would become so violently ill because of overindulging in a drink. Unfortunately, it wouldn't be the only, nor the last. All three of us recovered from the ordeal before morning. The good thing was that Margaret Ann wanted to tell Mom about the pillow fight and how Lillian and Dorothy chased us around the house. How we had a party, ate the chips and drinks. I was so lucky to have a talkative little sister this morning.

So, Mom never noticed my head lying on the table. My head was aching so much; my hair was praying for Joe the Barber to come and cut it free of this excruciating throbbing it was enduring.

As Mom looked around, she said. "Wow, looks like you enjoyed the Cream Soda."

As I made a beeline to the toilet, Lillian jumped out of my way.

I never had another sip, never mind a drink, of Cream Soda again. Even the thought or smell of Cream Soda returned me to that night when I learnt how to make my teeth chatter.

Joe the Barber

The small country hamlet of Terrebonne Heights was the home of some incredibly amusing characters in the 1950s. Each one would easily be subject enough for a novel. One such memorable character was "Joe the Barber."

Joe was one of those people that everyone in the village knew. Both from their personal experiences and, in my case, stories. Stories that I overheard from customers in my parent's store. Tales relating to minor mishaps and bleeding nicks from Joe's straight razor fully engaged my imagination as to what could happen behind that closed door of Joe's Barber Shop.

There was a small building near the corner of Brompton and English Roads, home to Joe's Barber Shop. It was about twenty feet by fifteen feet, with one door and two windows built on a foundation. A small wall divided the room, with the larger area housing Joe's barber's chair, a wall mirror, a counter where Joe stored his clippers and scissors, and a row of chairs along the wall. There was a small doorway leading to the second room. A curtain draped this doorway, for privacy, of Joe's wares.

I walked into Joe's shop with my dad, more like Dad dragged me in, trembling, with fear in my eyes and my heart trying to jump out of my chest. For even as a six-year-old, I had these images of stories overheard.

Joe was a big man, with a deep voice and a grin from ear to ear. Joe put me at ease as he picked me up and placed me on a bench across his barber's chair, giving me some extra needed height. Joe draped this apron around me and asked my dad what kind of haircut I wanted.

Over the years, I became aware that you could request any hairstyle, and Joe would always say, "Yep," and then give you the only cut he knew. A military regulation type of brush cut or, on special occasions, rumor has it, a "Mohawk," in the after-hours late on a Friday night.

Most, if not all, the men living in the Heights would go to Joe's for their haircut and get the latest news. While waiting their turn to clamber up into Joe's chair, you could hear them laughing at Joe's latest jokes.

Each of the men wanted to wait their turn. Every time Joe would duck behind the curtain to take another drink of beer, his shaking would lessen, as did the men's concern for their wellbeing.

I don't remember anyone answering, "Good," when Joe asked how their haircut looked. Most would act surprised, saying, "Not too bad, Joe," "Not too bad," "Not too shabby"; these men would get a haircut, a bottle or two of beer, some hilarious jokes, and the day's news for a dollar.

As kids, our parents would use the threat of having to see Joe for a haircut as a means of discipline if we didn't smarten up. I remember this one time of being sent to see Joe, and I would hide outside, waiting for some fathers to arrive. Then I would go in, knowing that Joe would get steadier while consuming his medicinal treatment with the passing of each haircut. Plus, if you remained quiet enough, you'd hear some adult jokes, like a sex education class.

One good thing about Joe's shaking was that his left hand and right hand were in perfect sync. So the hand holding your head matched the shaking of Joe's hand with the scissors or clippers.

Laughter, cigarette smoke, the aroma of beer, great stories, and the latest news were all part of Joe's Barber shop's atmosphere. Where I would learn a new cuss/swear word from time to time and the best jokes, as old Joe was also a great storyteller. He undoubtedly was also the "Terrebonne Height's Orator."

As I got older, Joe would start cleaning the hair around my neck and ears with a straight razor. Now I understood why those men needed a beer or two to build up their courage, and these were all men who had recently come home from the war. The first time I heard Joe utter these words was when he was using his straight razor, trimming up around my ears.

"Oops, don't worry about that, I've got something that will stop that bleeding." I envisioned seeing my severed ear falling to the floor.

On rare and special occasions, Joe's brother Bobby would drop in and start to sing together. Looking back today, I appreciate how well they sang. They would instantly turn Joe's Barber Shop into this beautiful music hall. This "Palais de la Musique" while making life-long memories.

Yes, Old Joe was my friend and all of us kids from the Heights.

Door to Door Delivery

Once the spring turned into summer, our little community would quickly grow, with all of the city folk starting to open up their summer cottages. Most would come to enjoy the absence of the constant turbulent clamor of a big city.

This infusion was considerable assistance, an asset, to the entrepreneurs in the Heights. Including not only people like my mom and dad's General Store, Paul Locas's Butcher/Grocery Shop, Bob Wood's Post Office/Grocery, and all of the other small business people in our area, Harry Joy's Supertest Garage, Art Kennel's Esso Station, Eddy Ellis's Garage Services.

There were also several vendors of note who delivered door to door during these warm weather months. While in no specific order, the ones that come to mind would be:

Johnny Aubien is a butcher who travelled from his shop in Mascouche to deliver his meat products in a large modified truck for this very purpose. There was a large roll cutter for the brown wrapping paper and a sizeable tapered spool of string suspended from the ceiling. I liked to watch when M. Aubien would wrap the meat in the wrapping paper, pull down some string, loop it around the package, and snap the string with his bare hands; it was really neat.

The truck's body was fitted with channeling, allowing the various available types of meat to slide while hanging from hooks. There was a chopping block that housed some eye-popping knives for a young boy like me. All glistening and seemed to be razor-sharp. Some had the appearance of a King's Excalibur.

I loved going with my mom when M. Aubien pulled up in front of our store and parked his big meat truck there while waiting for his customers in the area to come and shop. Big sides of beef would be hanging out the back of the truck, and there would be a cloud of flies constantly buzzing about, both M. Aubien and the meats.

M. Aubien always seemed to be in a good mood. I anxiously waited for M. Aubien to place the meats on the scale. The scale was white and had a large dial with an arrow-type pointer that would indicate the weight of the order.

Mom would always demand, "Johnny, you be sure to stand back from that scale."

So she could ensure that neither his big hand nor his thumb was on that scale. They both seemingly appeared to enjoy this exchange of mild insults and accusations. I think some people timed their shopping to watch this comedy exchange between my mom and Johnny.

Another welcome service was Mr. Poulin's. He also had a truck modified, to haul and display, his fresh selection of fruits and vegetables. He would travel throughout the village, going door to door. He too would park in front of our store, as we didn't carry much in this line of products, at this time of the store's development. Mr. Poulin was also a cheery fellow, usually with a smile on his face, and a few good stories to tell.

The meekest amongst these vendors was Mr. Cookson. He was the egg man for our community, Maybe with him being a meek and mannered individual, was indeed an asset when dealing with a fragile product, like eggs. Mr. Cookson delivered his fresh eggs once a week. He'd have his receipt book in one hand, then once he tallied the items, he would always lick his big fat pencil, before jotting the numbers down. He seemed to enjoy making time to have a chat with Mom, other than that, he gave the impression of being a very quiet man.

This was another characteristic, that perhaps wasn't evident during this time in the Heights. These vendors weren't only selling goods and services. They were connecting the surrounding communities with their stories, and the experiences that they encountered along the way. They provided the lifeline, a lifeline needed for smaller communities of the day, to continue to exist; by establishing a pulse, connecting each to one and other, in addition to tomorrow.

I remember waiting at our cottage, "Lucy," on Center Road, for the ice to be delivered. Mr. Partridge would jump out of his truck, waving to me while lifting the tarp, revealing the sawdust covering the ice. This sawdust would slow down the melting process.

He would place the ice right into the icebox that sat out on the front stoop. Large tongs would grab the ice, and I'd watch Mr. Partridge's arm muscles flex with this weight. With one hand, he would swing it up and into the icebox. Release the ice while shutting the door with his other hand. All in one motion. Very entertaining for a five-year-old boy to watch.

He'd walk past me sitting on the steps, tapping the peak of my cap and say.

"Have a good day, little knucklehead."

Neither of us could know at the time that this little 'knucklehead' would soon become a member of his partridge brood. This daily encounter began my long relationship with Fred, Mary Partridge, and the Partridge family.

Mr. Partridge would also deliver coal in the winter months to the permanent residences. In time, he would start supplying oil too. As more and more people made the switch to this newer heating source. One that was much more efficient, and cleaner, also requiring much less physical labor.

Another prominent legend of the Heights was Mr. Jimmy Robinson. And in due course, his mainstay is Bobby Leuty. Then, of course, there was Queenie, the mistress of the milk wagon.

Mr. Robinson was also very helpful to many of the young upstart families in the Heights. Besides owning "Jimmy's Beach," Mr. Robinson was our community milkman, delivering milk door to door throughout the year. Rain or shine, as well as in the snowstorms for which the Heights was famous.

The Robinson's lived on the north side of English Road, almost directly across from our store, great neighbors to have. Mr. Robinson also delivered milk to the area's three schools: the English Catholic, Holy Rosary School; the English Protestant, Lewis King School, and the French Catholic, Little White School House on top of the hill, on Garden Road. Seeing his milk truck drive up to the school before the start of lunch hour was always reassuring.

As the Heights started to grow, with more homes built and families continuing to have children, Jimmy decided to hire Bobby Leuty, among others, to deliver milk with a horse and wagon. A common sight would be to watch Queenie, clip-clopping along, hauling the old milk wagon, with Bobby asleep inside.

Then Queenie would stop up at the next delivery home. This stoppage would awaken Bobby, who would make the delivery and climb back into the milk wagon. Bobby would go back to sleep as Queenie headed to the next stop along the way. With the houses spaced far apart at the time, there was ample time for another snooze.

It indeed was a different time, a different era. One that, without doubt, is interconnected with the tempo of the 'clip-clop' of a horse's gait is a time never to be forgotten. A time that would not only be gone too soon but would be gone forever.

There were other types of services available in the Heights, as well. I clearly remember one my mother took full advantage of, as her working hours were always long and consuming.

Mrs. Haigh offered a laundry service out of her home on Rawlinson Road. Customers could drop off their soiled laundry and pick it up, cleaned, pressed, and folded in a day or two. With my mom's time constantly stretched to the limit, this cleaning service was a tremendous benefit. Mrs. Haigh's business was very recognized, as often, when I went to get mom's laundry, I would see others coming and going.

1949, The Great Fire

I was only three years old when my entire life's journey was threatened, obviously, unbeknownst to me. Eventually, all the kids living in the Heights at the time of the Great Fire would become aware of what our parents had experienced in August 1949.

I remember when Mom sat Margaret Ann and me down and related this incredible tale of extreme heroics and heroism.

"It started like any other day in August, and it ended with the chance of being one of the last we would ever spend in Terrebonne Heights."

She told me that at the time, the land in and around the Heights, and Terrebonne, was ninety percent agricultural farmland. The areas surrounding the Heights were primarily small family farms, as were the properties lying south, toward Mascouche. Consequentially, the Heights remained a young, mainly summer destination, a residential village with few local amenities.

Mom emphasized that this immensely wooded area surrounded the agricultural area, and this vulnerable and precarious location had become acutely evident with the fire at the end of August 1949.

How, the initial whiffs of smoke, with the distinct odor of wood-burning, had triggered her motherly senses of the foreboding perils that laid ahead.

Mom related how quickly this fire spread through these densely wooded areas as this fire continued to grow in both size and unpredictability. Mom and the other mothers were so grateful that many companies in and around Montréal were allowing their male employees living in the Heights to return home to combat this menacing blaze.

Fortunately, many of these men had recently spent time in one or more military combat outfits during the Second World War, training for such precarious conditions.

In combating this growing blaze, the Army soon arrived to help, bringing the much-needed equipment and expertise. Meanwhile, families were being gathered in front of the Legion's small ball field, awaiting transport out of the area. They were relocating most youngsters to Montréal.

I went to my grandparents in Pointe-Saint-Charles, and Margaret Ann, only one, remained with her. The women, and older girls, stayed to help by preparing and feeding the men for the duration of the fire.

In years to come, I would learn that the people in charge decided to create a credible firebreak north of the Heights. It would run parallel and just south of the Mascouche River. This two-mile-long fire break started at Moody Road and finished at Chemin Saint Marie.

This one-hundred-foot firebreak required the skills of the Military Engineers, the additional labor force made available, and the machinery, motivation, and Army personnel. With this decision and the fierce determination the Heights residents exhibited, the firebreak was ready to stand its final test.

I understand that the fire was eventually contained, but not before it left a large expanse of destruction and heartache. This fire burned over twenty cottages, and many more hectares of cherished woodland were either charred or destroyed.

I understand this was an epic battle, but I'm not sure of its duration, whether it entailed days or weeks. One individual, Mr. Mel Sullivan, was instrumental in his leadership role during this tragedy. Seventy-some-odd years later, it's easy to appreciate the whole course of Terrebonne Heights' future existence laid in the balance of these few weeks.

Then, in August of 1954, with another forest fire, the fear of history repeating itself, happening almost seven years to the day.

I was eight years old when Mom and Dad purchased "Moore's General Store," in the Heights.

At that time, the R.C.M.P provided police protection for the Heights. Mascouche, being a more populated village, had a full Fire Service. The travelling distance to the Heights impeded responding to any issue in the Heights within a reasonable time frame.

At this point in time, la Ville de Terrebonne had their own Police service "Service de police de Terrebonne" and their own fire protection service, "Service de sécurité d'incendie de Terrebonne," staffed trained Police Officers and Professional Firemen.

Consequentially, with Terrebonne Heights within the diocese of the Parish of Mascouche, it was outside the boundaries of Terrebonne. Therefore, at this point, there was no organized, professional fire service nor a volunteer fire service provided in the Heights. However, there was an acknowledgement by its citizens to assist when needed in the event of a fire.

Dad assumed the responsibility of maintaining the Community Fire Siren when purchasing his store, thus entrusting him with the task of alerting the community in the event of a fire. Once I was strong enough, it would become my responsibility to crank the 'siren' while warning the residents.

Someone calls the store in a panic, reporting a forest fire toward the end of Brompton Road. My dad grabs the siren while my mom starts phoning people. The good thing at the time was whenever the party line phones rang in the Heights, and it became a community call anyway. Everyone on that line would always pick it up, spreading the word quickly.

Dad drove, going road-by-road, alerting others. Men and older boys would be in hand outside their homes with shovels and axes. They were waiting to find out the location of the fire.

"Where's the fire, Sid?"

You could sense not so much the panic but the uneasiness of a feeling of déjà vu.

"Down the far end of Brompton Road, could be a big one."

Once they knew the location, pick-up trucks would be racing to the fire and picking up others heading there by foot. We, too, went to fight the fire when all the people were alerted. Okay, I wasn't allowed out of the truck, but I did have to guard the community's fire siren.

This forest fire, too, was ultimately contained, with far less destruction. Regardless, the anxiety was very relevant on people's faces.

For me to witness that problematic situation resolved by everyone pulling together and, significantly, in the same direction would often be drawn on in the years to come.

Changing of the Signs

In the mid-1950s, the "Moore's General Store" sign went up, replacing "Hart's General Store." One generation was ending with the next generation beginning. Hart's General Store was a very well-established business with an enviable reputation for serving the citizens of the Heights for many years. My parents, in time, would also achieve meeting, and in some ways, bettering, this high bar set by Mr. and Mrs. Hart.

"Moore's General Store,"
152 English Road,
Terrebonne Heights.
477-5566.
"NOW OPEN"

It seems like only yesterday, but in reality, it was a few 'lifetimes ago'. I still vividly recall all of those yesterdays, and those five wooden steps, leading up to the entrance to the store with a round iron hand railing on either side. The pitched roof over the entrance landing would provide some protection in inclement weather, with a half wall on either side. The front door was an oversized wooden door, one with a big brass bell suspended on a spring, that would announce your arrival.

On either side of the entrance was a six-foot-wide, four-sectioned glass window. These were a significant asset in allowing a good deal of unobstructed sunlight to stream in, creating a warm, friendly welcoming.

Upon entering, a full u-shaped counter bordered the ample open floor space. Very typical during this period. Behind the counters, I remember an array of wall units where the products were displayed and stored. A big friendly, wooden chair would greet you in the left corner when you entered. On this counter was the store's telephone. Where my mom would sit on her stool and jot down people's phone orders, often she could be found there chatting with whoever came in to place their order. My mom loved people, and they also seemed very fond of Mom.

Seriously, I don't ever recall seeing a man come in to purchase any grocery items, nor ever sit in that chair, come to think of it, a quirk of the times.

The counter on the left was the main area for grocery shopping, and the hardware materials would be available on the right side of the store. The counter space joining these two counters housed the glassed "penny candy" display, the main attraction to kids and moms alike.

The sight of these kids, with their two cents in hand, and their faces glued to the glass front of the penny-candy counter, were precious moments indeed. My mom was the "Fairy Godmother" and this was her Wonderland.

"Can I have one of those?"

"Yes."

"And one of those?"

"Yes."

Until that little brown candy bag was full, this was always the best part of the day for my mom. At the same time, my dad would shake his head and smile. Our dad loved our mom much more than he loved life itself.

All of us kids soon knew them by name; honeymoons, chocolate tools, black balls, green mint leaves, candy necklaces. That maple topped fudge cones, and who could forget the candy cigarettes. These were simpler times, with much simpler rewards, just for being a "Kid from the Heights."

The hardware was Dad's department. After a decade of being enlisted in the Navy, followed by nine years working at the Canadian Naval Supply Depot, Dad garnered a lot of knowledge and experience to draw on.

Below the counter, open boxes stored various sizes and types of nails. I remember that large weigh-scale with its balancing beam on the counter. Nails would be gathered in the metal cradle-shaped tray and placed on the scale. Nails could be scooped onto the tray using the raking device. I was always glad to pick up and sort the nails that ended up on the floor, as some seemed to follow me to where we were building our fort.

Also available were different styles and sizes of screws, nuts and bolts, either in small boxes or smaller quantities. Dad supplied some of the more common hardware tools too.

There was a three-foot-high gate, just to the right of the candy counter, with a small finger lock inside. This gate allowed passage behind the counter, which led to the entrance of the kitchen area of our home. The cigarettes were displayed and stored on the wall behind the candy counter. Cigarette sales made up a reasonable amount of the store's income, with nearly all adults taking up the habit. There were no 'legal' age restrictions at the time. It was popular to have a parent send one of their younger kids to pick up a package of cigarettes.

Directly below the cigarettes would have been the Coke cooler. Although it was called a "Coke" cooler, every kind of soft drink available at the time was there as well; Pepsi, Nesbitt's Orange in the brown bottles, Orange Crush, Gurds Ginger-ale, 7-Up, Snow White Cream Soda, Canada Dry Ginger Beer. Spruce Beer was also in brown bottles. There were also Mountain Dew and Hires Root Beer, among others.

These soft drinks came in a glass bottle, requiring a two-cent deposit and were available in both 7oz and 10oz sizes. The bottle manufacturers used a standard neck and top size, allowing these bottles to be suspended by their necks while remaining immersed in the cold water coolers.

The thing I remember most about opening a bottle of Coke back in the day were those extraordinary dense white gases that lingered inside the neck of the bottle, just floating around. The familiar sting of that first mouthful. I'm pretty sure Coke was the only one with this 'zest', when opened. I always looked forward to snapping that cap with a "Pop" and that misty aura.

A bottle opener on the side of the cooler had a long vertical receptacle where the caps would drop. I'd collect these bottle caps and save them for my friends for various projects.

The delivery/receiving area for the store was on the front, to the left of the building. A garage-style door, and a man door, allowed access to this storage area. This building was also where we would hide and smoke. The day Dad caught us, he told me that if I was going to smoke, I could do it in the house too. Now, this sort of ruined the intrigue of smoking for me. Oddly enough, I never smoked another day in my life. So, thanks, Dad, for loving me.

The store used this garage area for storing various soft-drink cases and other products. Toward the back, four steps led to another level where Dad kept the refrigeration units. Jimmy Robinson would deliver and place milk, butter, and some cheddar cheeses in there. Also, when providing his flats of eggs, Mr. Routhier would use this landing area. This area's entrance was direct across from the stairs leading to the basement, where more hardware services were available.

One section of the basement housed the pipe cutting and threading machine, including the various sizes and lengths of pipes and fittings. Adjacent to this area was a sizeable glass-cutting table with a vast assortment of glass.

Often old man Wells would come into the store muttering, "That it was too damn cold in the mornings, for this time of the year."

Once Dad finished cutting and threading the plumbing materials he needed. Mr. Wells would back his truck up to the loading area, and often you could hear him say, "Lord have mercy, it's going to be a hot one today."

He always covered both sides of the argument 'well', no pun intended.

Most of the remaining basement area had shelved units for storing canned goods and non-perishable items until required upstairs. Rather than carrying anything upstairs, Dad created an opening giving access to the store level.

The cash register's location remained at the end of the grocery counter, where it met the candy display. Sales from both hardware and grocery items used this register.

However, the most purposeful item in the store was the big wooden drawer below the counter, near where my mom sat. This drawer housed all of the receipt books containing customers' credits. Recording daily purchases for each family with the expectation that they would pay at the month's end.

Smaller daily purchases were usually cash sales, but larger grocery orders could be on credit. This option was unavailable to hardware sales; I'm not sure why, but that's how it was.

There was always the option to phone in and have Mom write out your order for delivery. Then, it would be filled and boxed, waiting for Dad to make the delivery. Another, more common option was for the women of the household to come to the store with their shopping list. While sitting and talking to Mom as she filled out the order. Most often, these women would take what was needed immediately, with the remainder delivered later.

Most customers would place two or three small orders in any given week rather than one large order. There were a few exceptions, where one large order would be required. Regardless of size, all would be delivered.

I always liked it when Mrs. Joy would walk down from their Supertest garage with her dog "Spot." He would wait patiently for his can of dog food and, with it in his mouth, headed home alongside Mrs. Joy.

There was a Bell Canada payphone booth outside the front of the store, and very convenient in the early 50s to mid 60s, with telephones still considered a luxury to most people. The store was also a stop for the Provincial Bus, allowing passengers to get off on their way home from work.

The store was a two-story design with a large full basement. The front portion of the first floor was the store itself. Behind this area were our family's living quarters. Starting with the kitchen, this adjacent location to the kitchen to the store was crucial back in the days of these small country general stores.

Another area of the main floor was a nice-sized family room. Then, a short hall led to the house's front door. At this entrance, there were stairs leading to the upper floor. Three bedrooms were located upstairs, along with a full-sized bathroom. These four rooms encompassed the landing, an open hall area providing additional storage space. All three bedrooms and the bathroom on this upper floor were significant for this period.

This building radiated a warm, friendly ambience, whatever the season, especially during the winter. The heating system consisted of a sizeable oil-fired furnace integrating a hot water radiator system, with large radiators installed in every room. These radiators would need periodic draining to keep them from getting air-locked, restricting the hot water flow through them. Each Saturday morning during the heating season, it would be my job to release the air from each unit by opening a valve at the base of each radiator. Accepting these responsibilities at this young age prepared my steadfast approach to finding a resolution to my life's issues.

The roof was 'barn' shaped, not the standard steep slope roofs more commonly found in this region of Québec. My dad had a steel roof installed, hoping that snow would more readily slide off compared to the previous asphalt shingles.

The final room on the first level was at the rear of the house and was for storing various drummed fuels; coal oil, kerosene, turpentine and other solvents. There was a workshop located at the back of this good-sized backyard. A small stream bordered the back of the yard.

The store would open at eight am, six days a week, closing at nine pm. Other than Tuesday, when it would close at two in the afternoon. The store was never opened on Sunday and would close at eleven pm on Friday and Saturday in the summer months.

I was about to experience a much different existence than most boys my age, gaining experiences and knowledge that would serve me well in the years ahead.

Oh, one more thing, my dad would usually sign some blank cheques whenever he would be away from the store. In case something like a delivery, or such, is being made in his absence.

Then one day, it happened, delivery and no signed cheques. I was drawing in my sketchbook at the kitchen table when Mom came with the checkbook and a cancelled cheque. Knowing that I was conscious of details, she put both on the table, saying, "Copy Dad's signature."

"That's forgery Mom," I quipped.

Wow, please give me that checkbook. I'm thinking now that I should have drawn and written a comic book about a Super Hero, the Terrebonne Heights Forger.

As their customer base grew, so did the opportunity for Mom and Dad to hire more staff at the store. Mom hired Mrs. Dawe and my cousin Dorothy to assist her in the store. Victor Bennett was employed to make deliveries and help with restocking and general duties in and around the store.

Margaret Ann and I were so thankful when Dorothy worked in the store and started preparing meals and making our school lunches. Before this, mom's school lunch specialty was a peanut butter sandwich and a box of Sun Maid raisins.

The Early Years

When you're a nine-year-old boy and your parents own a general country store, chores are always waiting. I remember my first chore was sorting the various soft drink empties people returned for credit and placing them into their wooden return crates. There were some intriguing shapes and colors, which made it easier to identify them for sorting.

At the time, you could purchase a six-pack carton of seven-ounce Coke for thirty-six cents, and '6 for 36' was printed on these cartons. This sorting chore would be the beginning of my day. I remember that my little sister Margaret Ann had no tasks at this time.

My next job was putting the eggs into the 'dozen eggs' boxes; the eggs came in a big wooden box of five flats. With twenty-five eggs per flat, one hundred and twenty-five eggs per box. What an odd number when you're dealing in dozens. I seem to remember that my younger, blonde-haired sister still had no chores at this time.

Moving on, I graduated to restocking shelves. Mom would make an inventory list of what needed restocking. I would go downstairs, and with the use of an old wooden box for the extra height I needed, I could toss these items through the opening to the store's floor level. Then go upstairs and refill the empty shelves. Once again, I vaguely remember that my blue-eyed, pretty little blonde-haired sister, had no chores at this time.

When I was eleven, my dad successfully taught me how to operate the large pipe treading and cutting machine. He explained the necessity of proper lubrication when cutting galvanized pipes and patience when using the treading devices. I enjoyed the fact that Dad trusted me with these responsibilities.

I often watched my dad cutting glass to size and, at times to shape. My dad was a master glass-cutter, to the point of being able to cut circles in the glass. He taught me the differences between single and double diamond glass and the cutting techniques. I mastered none and could break either single or double diamond glass equally well. It didn't matter.

Although I enjoyed working on that big glass-cutting table, the only thing I got good at was throwing the broken pieces into the big bin below the table. My younger, I'm sure you're starting to get the picture here. Margaret Ann enjoyed being Dad's Little Princess, who had an enviable position in life. Then again, I always felt that Margaret Ann would have preferred to be more of a "Ragged-Ann-Doll," and down off that pedestal, well, maybe only partially down, but a little bit.

One of the store's many perks was the added financial opportunities. For instance, when my dad was busy with his deliveries, someone required pipe cutting and threading. My mom would tell them to go to the ball field and ask for Skipper, "See if he'll cut the pipe for you."

My dad charged twenty-five cents per cut and thread; I, on the other hand, would tell them that I charged fifty cents.

"What…50¢…it's only 25¢, it's always been 25¢."

Me: "At the store when Dad does it, yes, but not today, Dad's away and if you want me to do it for you, it's 50¢."

"Your dad will be hearing about this, damn Highway Robbery this is, I tell you, Highway Robbery."

They would all grumble and growl until I would mention, "What a fine day it was for 'kids' to be playing ball."

In the end, they always thanked me, probably remembering some things they missed out on during their youth. These customers would always grumble to Dad on their next visit. But usually added when finished, "That boy's going to do just fine in life Sid, just fine."

Another thing that Gilles and I did was sell soft drinks anytime there was a game at the Baseball field. We'd put a big metal tub on my delivery wagon, the one with those wide air-filled tires. Once we loaded the tub with soft drinks and cold water, we'd haul it to the baseball field.

We paid Mom seven cents a bottle, promising to return all the empty bottles. Then we sold the soft drinks for fifteen cents, including the two-cent deposit for the bottle. So doing the math, we made six cents a bottle and charged three cents for the return.

Gilles was our "Ringmaster" as he cried out, "Cold drinks…ice-cold drinks."

"…Get your cold drinks here."

"…Cold drinks."

Then shortly, he'd attract more customers with:

"Boissons froides."

"Boissons glacées."

"Achetez vos boissons fraîches ici."

"Boissons fraîches."

Gilles would pay some kids to go around during the day and after the final game to gather up all the empties. He would pay them two cents a bottle. Bottles that we would return to the store, then sort them.

Because we hadn't yet paid Mom for the bottles, we needed to return the empties to her. So we matched the two cents the kids would have if they had returned the bottles to one of the local stores. Besides, the kids could do this during the games while we were busy selling drinks. We were keeping them out of mischief while leaving a lot less for us to pick up at the end of the day.

We would split the six cents a bottle profit that we made. Although we only used cold water, we advertised "Ice Cold Drinks," and if people asked about the lack of ice, we'd say it melted.

My parents worked hard their entire lives, as did most parents of the day, to make a better life for my sister and me. Attested by the store opening at 8:00 am. six mornings a week.

The store closed early Tuesday afternoons allowing my parents time to complete the daily bookkeeping tasks before heading out to a night of bowling. Tuesday Night Bowling was all the rage, with about half of the other parents in the Heights participating. Other than this one evening, the store would remain open until 9:00 pm nightly, changing to 11:00 pm on Fridays and Saturdays during the summer.

A delivery truck drove up to the store on one particular Tuesday evening, just weeks before Christmas. We weren't to accept any deliveries while our parents were out bowling, but I noticed that this wasn't the regular delivery service. So, while enduring my little sister's trumpeted threats, I asked the driver to see the invoice.

I told him I'd open the doors for him to make his delivery. My little sister nagged me all the way, suggesting how much trouble was ahead for me.

"You just wait until Mom and Dad get home, you're in big troubles mister, big, big, trouble."

That was until she saw this beautiful big toboggan coming through the doorway. The remainder of our Christmas presents followed it.

"Ooooh."

Many items were in larger corrugated boxes, and the invoice for these items was still inside. So, we didn't know every gift we might be getting but hoped the more oversized items wouldn't be for sale in the store.

I think this was the same Christmas when we were heading to bed on Christmas Eve that I told Margaret Ann, "If she fell asleep, the 'evil spook' would make her sleep right through Christmas Day."

About an hour later, as my bedroom door flew open, I knew my dad was not impressed with my visionary abilities. He told me, "That he too was somewhat of a visionary. And if I continued tormenting little Miss Goody Two Shoes."

Maybe he didn't say little Miss Goody Two Shoes, but the message was clear.

My dad's "bark" was a healthy one, but his bite, on the other hand, was more like a "STOP" sign in Québec, only a suggestion at best.

During this period, I would make deliveries pulling my wagon, the one with the big rubber inflatable tires, and in the winter months, I used a sleigh.

I got to meet, and know, a lot of fascinating, unique characters. Watching as they overcame their struggles, the ingenuity displayed at times was quite impressive. But the best perk was getting to know the people and having them get to know me, too.

Which reminds me, no "pun" intended. Back in the 50s, every country village had a haunted house. Or at least a witch lived in a deep overgrown, vine-infested, creepy house. One that was full of cats, most being black. The Heights was to be no exception.

There happened to be one such house in the Heights situated on Poplar Road, just down from the corner of English Road. Without a 'shadow' of doubt, with creeping vines and two feet of high-uncut grass. Rumor had it that a plague of cats infested this old, dilapidated house, most of them being black.

Serge told me, "That a friend of his told a friend of Gilles that their friend had almost definitely, seen with their own eyes. The old women living there turn a frog into a snake."

So she had to be a witch. This evolution would make perfect logic for an eleven-year-old boy. I think he probably witnessed a snake eating a frog, but this wouldn't be such a compelling tale to tell.

This house was a little creepy by being overrun with vines. She had an awful lot of cats. I knew for a fact about the cats as my dad would make a delivery once a week to Mrs. Medcafe. I was the one who helped Mom put the order together and then packed it in boxes for delivery. Every week the order would have at least ten cans of cat food. That's a lot of cat food.

When I mentioned the cans of cat food to the guys, that sealed the deal right then and there. Only a witch would need all of that cat food.

Then it happened, Dad had already made the delivery to Mrs. Medcafe, but she had missed ordering a bag of flour.

"Don't worry, Mrs. Medcafe, and Skipper will bring it over."

The odds weren't good that there might be two Skippers, so I told Mom that it was getting dark for me to walk over there.

"Where are you looking?" Mom said.

I walked over, hoping to meet a friend along the way. There wasn't one other person anywhere. As I approached the house, it seemed to be back quite a bit further off the road, more than I remembered and seemed drearier.

I nervously knocked on the door, waiting, but no one answered. I looked around, noticing at least one cat in every window. Still, nobody answered the door. Now I think I'll come back tomorrow in the daylight when spooks aren't around. Mom said to go in and put it on her table if she didn't come to the door, as she was hard of hearing.

Being so poorly lit, it was eerie, really, but I could see the kitchen table. In a cold sweat, I stepped forward to put the flour on the table, and I stepped on a cat's tail. All hell broke loose. Like a shot out of hell, this petrified cat and at least a dozen others were screeching like terrified Banshee and jumping as though something had stuck their tails into an electrical outlet while emitting this loathing motherload of 'hissing and spitting'.

Mrs. Medcafe screamed, a terrifying, death-defying, shrill.

I threw the flour so violently into the air it exploded when hitting the ceiling, now showering the entire kitchen, Mrs. Medcafe and me, with flour. We were, without doubt, as white as ghosts.

This witch turned out to have a great sense of humor and hilarious laughter. It, too, was contagious. She was laughing so much that she started snorting through her nose. My laughter, on the other hand, was fear-based.

Things settled back as Mrs. Medcafe told me it had been years since she had laughed so openly, too many years. As I helped her vacuum up the flour and cleaned up the kitchen, she started laughing again, saying, "I've got a lot of white cats now." I started to like Mrs. Medcafe.

Before I left, she asked me if my friends, too, thought that she might be a witch?

"Well, then," she said, "perhaps you could not mention, that I'm not a witch."

As she added, it seemed that this incident had rekindled her naughty side.

"It could be, I'll start boiling water outside, in a big old black cast-iron pot, and speak with a vexing witches voice. Whenever I see any of your friends lurking about."

It surely warrants repeating. As I made my deliveries, it was so much fun to get to know the people of the Heights, yes, even the witches.

Stormy and Things Around the Kitchen

It was a miserable night, as strong winds accompanied the torrential rains; the night, I drove with my dad to a little village just east of Ste. Therese, Québec. We were on our way to retrieve dad's German Shepherd pup. I had begged Dad for a dog since we moved into the store.

"Dad, Granddad said that a boy should grow up with a dog, and a dog should grow up with a boy. I think it's time that you too started to listen to your dad, don't you."

Dad: "Remind me to have a word with your Grandfather."

I'm not sure if I persuaded Dad with my logic, but we were now on the way to completing my dream.

A small, slightly balding man eager to show my dad the litter greeted us. My dad had the pick of the litter, so once decided, the remainder of this purebred litter would be available for sale.

My dad seemed to know a lot about selecting a pup. I remember that he brought a wooden yardstick with him. As the puppies were playing about, Dad held the yardstick with the front of his foot. He started to pull it toward himself, causing stress on the yardstick. Then let it slip from his grasp, releasing the pent-up pressure, caused the yardstick to make a slight slapping sound when it made contact with the wooden floor.

Some pups didn't react much, but others scattered, becoming eliminated. Dad had three or four other "tests," which elude my memory today; eventually, my dad and his pup were united.

The pup was tattooed around the belly area. Then some official-looking forms were filled out and signed. Dad told me not to be touching his ears as the small cartilage in the ears could easily be broken at this stage of development. This contact could result in disfigurement of the ear.

The official name of the pup was something like, "The Vice-Regal Storm of Terrebonne," I called him Stormy. It indeed suited the night we went to pick him up.

I so desperately wanted to hold Stormy on the drive home and was trying to think of a way to convince Dad when I noticed that Dad never brought an empty box. My dad had already planned my dream to become a reality. I loved my dad. So yes, that night I got to hold Stormy on the way home, I was in heaven.

Stormy was, without question, my dad's dog. They just loved each other, with the bond being instantaneous and deeply seeded between them.

Dad took the necessary time to develop their mutual trust and showed me how to use a German choker chain in the training process. How the blunt prongs of the chain only pinched the neck, not as many people believed that those sharp spikes would savagely cause harm to the dog. When not in a training session, Dad would invert this same collar. When reversed, the collar would protect the dog's neck from attack from any source, animal or human.

My dad also had a fondness for Budgie Birds, usually having two or three at any given time. He would allow these birds to fly freely about the kitchen. When they noticed that Stormy was sleeping on the floor, they would land on the floor, some distance away, waiting for Stormy to close his eyes again. Once they sensed an opportunity, they would inch forward whenever Stormy closed his eyes, getting closer, until they'd make their move and give Stormy a peck on the nose.

Up would jump Stormy, and this would throw the kitchen table flying. The budgies would return to the safety of their cage. One day I envisioned coming home to find Stormy with a mouth full of Budgie feathers if they kept this up.

Then the next step in their entertainment was to work as a team. The birds were landing on the table and watching Stormy trying to sleep, alongside the old radiator, near the table. Stormy was aware of their presence, usually watching from the corner of one eye. They would continually push a teaspoon while checking on Stormy's location. It was impressive how persistent and precise they were, generally ending with the same result. The spoon lands on Stormy, and the table goes flying.

In the summer months, Mom would go to war with those pesky house flies by suspending 'fly catchers' from the kitchen ceiling. The ones you'd push the tack into the ceiling, then it uncoiled as you pulled on it. The coating on the strip was this sticky mess of something or other to catch any house flies that landed or even touched the surface. Well, they captured more than flies. They managed to catch dad's Budgie birds with no trouble whatsoever.

My well-known so-called; cold-hearted dad would be gently washing his budgies in the kitchen sink with detergent and warm water. Slowly, gently coaxing the gooey mess out of their fragile feathers. Watching our Dad do this was a sight for both Margaret Ann and me. As for without these budgies, we would have never seen this side of our dad. Dad was a firm believer in the position of authority, the obligation of respect, and an orderly process executed and followed.

For example, each Sunday, we would walk to church. Upon returning home, we could do what we wanted in our rooms until dinner, expected at the table at two o'clock. I would be wearing a white shirt and tie, and Margaret Ann would be in her dress. It was the tradition that someone would say a Grace before every weekday evening supper meal and at Sunday's more formal afternoon dinner. There was to be no laughing and no elbows on the table at this dinner meal, or you would be leaving the table for your room.

This expectation was never a problem for us. That was until our cousin Arthur would come to stay with us for the summer. Arthur was a tall, skinny kid, always had a brush-cut and wore thick glasses. And at his young age, he could be rated up there as one of the most uncoordinated kids in the entire world.

For example, Arthur would be eating peas, picking them up with a spoon. When lifting the spoon to his mouth, it would inevitably catch the edge of something. Arthur would continue trying to raise the spoon until suddenly, it would break free, and with this pent-up pressure released. The peas would look like Haley's comet passing through our kitchen.

At times, he would be drinking milk and suddenly start laughing about Gawd knows what. Then there would be milk spraying everywhere, with some frequently spewing out of his nose. Other times we'd be sitting at the table when suddenly Arthur would unexplainably look like a test pilot ejecting from the cockpit seat of a jet in intense distress, falling from his chair with his arms and legs rapidly flailing in the air. Then he would pick up his chair and sit down again as if nothing had ever happened. Seriously, how is anyone supposed to not react to something this hilarious?

Yes, Margaret Ann and I missed a lot of Sunday meals. Margaret Ann tried so hard not to look at him, or in his general direction, to no avail as she would catch something out of the corner of her eye and soon get up from her chair and head upstairs.

When Arthur came for the summer, it was like living in a vaudeville show for months. When he went home to Montréal for school in September, it got so quiet at the dinner table. We couldn't wait for his return next July.

During the school year, our Aunty Chick, Arthur's mom, would often call to report what bone Arthur had recently broken and how. They lived in Montréal, on Aylmer Street, a street that had a very steep incline and was always a concern to walk along at the best of times. Arthur was on his way to school, walking down Aylmer Street and lost his balance. The more he tried to regain his balance, the more any chance of recovery faded. With his long legs taking longer and longer strides, Arthur was in full flight when reaching the end of Aylmer Street and ran into the side of a city bus travelling along Milton Street. Believe it or not, he went right through the back doors of the bus, where you can either get on or off the bus. Fortunately, the Royal Victoria Hospital location was on Pine Avenue, at the top of Aylmer. Yep, cousin Arthur broke his collarbone again.

Another oddity regarding Arthur was the attraction he had for mosquitoes. The Heights being the perfect breeding grounds for the mass spawning of mosquitoes, there was never any shortage. The nightly reenactment of the Battle of Britain was a testament to their tenacity as they continuously buzz-bombed their sleeping victims. Going in my ear was the worst feeling. Arthur was like Peanut's character Pig-Pen with his cloud of dust, but Arthurs was mosquitoes. No one else would need to fend off the little pests when Arthur was around. There always seemed to be someone that was a homing beacon for these pesky mozzie Nighthawks.

I told Arthur that it was because he had "city blood," being born in the city, living in the city, going to school in the city and playing in the city; there was no doubt that he had city blood and mosquitoes craved city blood.

As it turned out, Art became one of the finest guitar players I ever had the pleasure of listening to, and his voice was the perfect complement to his playing. Art went from being a caterpillar to a distinct butterfly.

Although cooking wasn't mom's forte, she did make the best French Fries. Mom had one of those wall units for slicing whole potatoes into fries. I would struggle to pull that long handle, forcing the potato through the cutter blades, but Mom always let me try anyway. If they were 'new' potatoes, then after slicing the potatoes, Mom would parboil them for a minute to pre-soften them before putting them into her deep fryer of cooking oil. The 'old' potatoes would get a quick dip into the boiling water to remove some of the starch associated with old potatoes.

If someone entered the store, mom would go to wait on them, and I would keep slicing potatoes. Sometimes, Mom would sit absentmindedly on her stool out in the store and talk to whomever she had just served. I learned that a whole bag of sliced potatoes was too many potatoes. So, if I cut too many potatoes, Mom would keep them submerged in water in the fridge, so they wouldn't turn black until Mom fried them.

The time my dad bought our mom a pressure cooker. My mom's secret "family recipes" included canned and packaged products with lots of pots, only boiling water containing nothing but water. Boiling water in itself was not a simple task for our mom. We were lucky to have our cousin Dorothy working at the store, as she also prepared most of our meals.

This iron monster arrived in our kitchen in the spring of the year. I was upstairs with my sketchpad drawing. My mom always encouraged me with my artistic interests. My dad never was a big fan of the liberal arts; he accepted it but never encouraged me.

Suddenly there was this massive explosion downstairs. As I'm peering through this cloud of steamy smatterings of what was once food, I see my mom on the floor.

Me: "Are you all right Mom?"

Mom: "Come and look at this on the ceiling."

"Doesn't it look like a tree?"

Somehow, I didn't think my father would see this tree, especially on this freshly painted ceiling. My father asked what happened, and Mom calmly said, "That she didn't think this pot was cooking anything."

"So I opened it to check."

It wouldn't surprise me to discover that the creators of "I Love Lucy" followed my mom around, taking notes for their following script. It really wouldn't.

Shortly after this incident, purely coincidental I'm sure, the manufacturers and pressure cookers' makers installed a locking device, preventing anyone from opening these units while they were still under pressure.

I think my dad took what remained of this pressure cooker outside and buried it. Even today, I question what Dad could have been thinking about purchasing this pressure cooker for our mom. Then again, if our mom asked for it, Mom got it.

Dad obviously, adored our mom.

By the way, he never could remove those tree stains from the kitchen ceiling altogether.

The Beer License

In the late 50s, Dad sold the hardware section of Moore's General Store to Mr. Ted Morris. Mr. Morris soon opened his hardware store on Joy Road.

With the removal of the hardware section, my parents converted the store to a serve-yourself style, with isles rather than a generally open area. They did this redesign in preparation for applying for a Provincial Beer Permit. This application would become a long-drawn-out process involving many bureaucratic agencies within the Société des alcools du Québec.

My parents and Mr. and Mrs. Paul Locas (of Locas' Butcher/Grocery situated on Joy Road) simultaneously applied for these permits. After gaining approval from all of the required agencies, a community held a referendum with positive results. Even with the Société des alcools du Québec giving its blessing, there was yet, one more needed signature. And without Father LaLande's, our local Catholic Priest's blessings, all was for not. His coveted signature would assure the ratification of these applications.

Father Lalande said, "He was pleased to award both of these entrepreneurs their respective Beer Licenses. Recognizing their continuing contribution, sponsorship, and continuing endorsement of both, Religious and Social Activities in Terrebonne Heights."

Reading between the lines, I think that this was Father LaLande's way of thanking both families for their constant monitory support of the church's "Saturday Night Bingo."

This expansion again required modifications to our store; More coolers and more storage area for the beer while needing a significant space for the anticipated bottle handling. Fortunately, the beer bottles were all uniform sizes and could be returned to any brewery, regardless of label.

This expansion significantly increased the store's volume of business, especially on the weekends. However, one consequential restriction within the permit was one that the Société des alcools du Québec closely monitored. You were not permitted to deliver beer alone, delivery was not permissible without a food purchase with the order.

So the store is now open until 11:00 pm on Friday and Saturday nights. There was more bread sold between the hours of 9:00 to 11:00, than just about during any regular weekday hours. With so many ordering a case of beer and a loaf of bread, I guess 'Moore's General Store' was one of the first "B&B's" in the area.

The community, as a whole, benefited from all of these expansions. Mr. Morris was able to develop and grow his hardware business. There would be more than enough population to support both stores selling beer.

It's worth noting that there was no credit available for beer purchases. Rightfully, some were concerned about a negative impact with the ready availability to purchase beer locally. Fortunately, this was mainly unfounded, evidenced by the increased food sales. The general population seemed to be acting responsibly.

The profit margins also improved, enabling my parents to employ additional staff. Removing all the pipe threading and glass cutting equipment from the basement allowed for more shelving space helping other varieties of products to be made available and a broader selection of brand names. It was so rewarding to see that all these years of my parent's hard work finally started to pay dividends.

The Vermettes

In 1954, my parents, Sid and Dolly Moore, purchased Harts General Store, renaming it Moore's General Store, located at the intersection of English and Maple roads. This move was the next chapter in my young life, of delight and heartache.

The Heights was starting to 'become of age' as more veterans purchased land here and built homes while establishing families. Many veterans arrived with their new wives and some with a small family in tow. They were looking for a piece of land and some building materials.

They arrived with meagre means and pockets full of hope and energy. These newcomers rolled up their sleeves and continuously wiped the sweat from their brows with the determination to create a new life. The Heights was awakening.

One such family was the Vermette family. They lived down toward the end of Maple Road, on the left side of the road. Their home was just across from the Brisebois family. Like most people in the Heights, their home, too, was being built board-by-board and nail-by-nail whenever materials became available.

Mom called out, "Where are you going with that hammer, young man."

Me: "I'm going down to the Vermette's to help Gilles."

Mom: "Okay, but be back before it gets dark…and do you have clean underwear on, just in case you're in an accident?"

I never understood this reasoning because it won't be clean for long if I'm in an accident.

Me: "Yes, Mom, it's clean."

Mom: "Show me...Donald, they're not clean, where did you get them?"

Me: "In the hamper, where you put them."

Now heading to the Vermettes, with a hammer in hand, and clean underwear on, to help my best friend, Gilles. This trait was another unique experience about the Heights. Whoever you played with at the time was your "Best Friend," regardless of the number. If there were two, three, or more, all were your best friend.

Walking along Maple Road on this warm spring morning, there was magic in the air, especially when you're ten and on your way to help a friend out. The muddy early spring roads were now drying up. There were fewer wooden planks and boards along people's walkways leading to their front doors. Still, lots of signs when the thaw was at its peak bogging down cars last week, with the frost rapidly melting, and muddy roads were consuming vehicles at will, like quicksand.

Last week when I was walking to help Gilles, I watched all the clothes drying in the sun while suspended from the clotheslines. Most people would have a long thin wooden pole placed in the middle of the clothesline to support the line, keeping the freshly washed items from reaching the ground. The wind would sway the clothesline back and forth, pivoting on this post, as the shirts, dresses and pants nonchalantly dance. As I passed Mrs. Slade's home, her young pup was yapping and chasing these trespassers beside her house.

The presence of everyone's clean wash on their clotheslines was a definite sign that spring had arrived after a long winter of laundry done indoors and then put out on the clothesline. The frozen shirts and pants on the line would look like rigid stick people during winter. The aspect of bed linens being dried outdoors in the fresh spring air was a welcomed change.

I'd help Mom bring in the clothes from the line and later change all of the bedding. Mom showed me how to make the bed and fold the sheets, especially the fitted ones. Sometimes I would lay between the sheets inhaling this fresh air aroma. I'm sure that the air on the moon is the same as sheets when they're dried outdoors in the spring.

The birds were returning, and the trees were budding up. There was still lots of water in the ditches, so I stopped to check on the frogs a few times. Some of the potholes were pretty deep and full of water. One was over my knees, but it never reached my clean underwear. Although I got a soaker, my Billy boots made this sloshing sound as I continued walking to Gilles. Life was good.

Dick and Gilles had already started straightening nails as I arrived, and they told me that Serge would be late. Serge was usually late, as his dad seemed to give him the more time-consuming chores to do. Plus, Serge had just started a paper route delivering the Gazette. Yes, he would begin making his deliveries around 5:00 am, be home, washed and changed, and be ready to head off to school by 8:00 am.

Even at this young age, certain traits were becoming evident and apparent. Gilles was the risk-taker among us, a daredevil of sorts; he was always up to any challenge. He was also kindhearted and a real charmer.

Serge was the dreamer of the group and probably the most sensitive as well. Friends loved it when I would make him laugh by telling jokes as he would slowly build from a faint, almost inaudible giggle to a resounding, gut-busting outburst of laughter.

Dickie was already showing signs of his organizational abilities and compulsion to document events. He had all the storage sorting tins numbered and in sequence as to their sizes, and God forbid any of us to get them out of order. It was easy to envision Dickie becoming an Ambassador in his adult life.

This synopsis brings us to me. Likewise, with my nickname Skipper, I mirrored it by being a leader in nearly everything I encountered. Not by choice; things just seemed to find me somehow. I was also the jokester, loving a good prank or telling a good story, and there have been suggestions that sometimes I might have stretched the facts a little. As the years went on, frequently bounded about was the word embellishment.

Today the old metal bucket was crammed to the brim, with bent and rusty nails of every imaginable description. As usual, sometimes we'd sit around an old Maple tree stump or on the back steps of the house with our hammers. Straightening, as well as sorting nails. Common nails, finishing nails, and a tin can for each of the different lengths.

It was so much fun for us to be doing this while helping Gilles. It would be different if I were doing this at home. How is it things at home are chores, the same thing at friends is always fun? A sure sign of how life would soon be getting more complicated.

Once we had finished the day's chore, we would play for the rest of the day. Madame Vermette would make sandwiches and Kool-Aid for all of us. And then, we'd be either making some bows and arrows or some wooden toy rifles. Ever since the day Gilles's grandfather, M. Barrette, saw us playing cowboys and Indians while shooting at each other, we were now only allowed to be either cowboys 'or' Indians.

On this day, we would make our homemade toy rifles because the last days were good days for drying clothes outdoors. Everyone had a bag of clothes pegs used to hold their clothes on their clotheslines. Also, we could find some pegs on the clothesline which was too high for us to reach. So, we would look in these bags for damaged or broken pegs. While removing these suspected damaged pegs, we would perhaps, take a much-needed good peg or two. These pegs would become the main component of our rifles. We would use a three-foot-long piece of 1" x 2" old board for the rifle stock and barrel.

Take a small finishing nail to attach an undamaged peg to the butt end and another finishing nail inserted at the end of the barrel. Often the peg would split when we nailed it to the stock. But one day, Gilles accidentally had the nail upside down, and after hitting the sharp end once, he turned it over, and the peg didn't split. Our first experience with the mother of invention theory (blunt the point first, and the wood won't break).

We would remove and keep the spring part of the broken/damaged pegs, as these would become our ammo. I would save up the elastics that I could find around the store. These elastic bands would be looped and attached to the springs that came from the damaged clothes pegs. The looped end would go over the nail at the end of the barrel with the elastic bands stretching the wooden barrel's length. We would put the spring into the gap of the good clothes peg. The rifle is now loaded and ready for action.

Once fully armed, then stationed at strategic positions around the Vermette household in defense of invaders. Sometimes coming from Mascouche, sometimes Aliens, other times from an Indian attack.

On this occasion, Pirates were attacking. They were storming out of the gullies with swords in hand, and some were on wooden peg legs. This encounter would be the most brutal battle we had ever endured, as they were much quicker on those wooden peg legs than our Captain Gilles anticipated. Madame Vermette saved us by telling us it was time to go home before it got dark. But we all agreed, before parting for the day, that we had those nasty old Pirates running scared.

Dick, Serge and I headed home. We were tired out from the chores completed, as well as surviving such an epic battle. We said goodbye to Dick first, as his home was just down the road from the Vermette's. It was a relief to see that the house lights weren't on yet.

Serge and I continued down Maple while reliving some of the more legendary moments during the "Siege of Vermette."

I said, "so long," to Serge when we got to the store, as his home was still a little further along English Road.

So here I am, arriving home with dried Billy boots, clean underwear, and a fantastic Pirates tale to tell my mom.

She always breathlessly waited to hear all the exciting details. I had the best mom ever.

1957

October was always a month where weather prediction was, at best, a guess. The boards for the hockey rink needed erecting before the ground was too severely frozen. A small crew of men, and most boys my age, would assemble at the Mascouche Community Club grounds on the morning, where the rink was to be situated.

The walls of a hockey rink are "the boards." With each section being ten feet in length and forty-two inches in height. The ice surface would be 200 feet long and 85 feet wide.

The rink sides are ninety degrees to the surface of the rink. Serge's eldest brother, Jean Pierre, would lay out the corner posts using the Pythagorean theorem, ensuring perfect alignment of the rink.

This would be the first year we would have round corners, rather than each corner being at 45 a degree angle. A 2" x 4" brace supported these bolting sections on the exterior side with an anchor post, driven deep into the ground. Now we waited for below-freezing temperatures to flood the surface.

Many men and women of the community helped with clearing the snow from the hockey rink's surface, assuring that we would be able to play. Several men also assisted with the watering of the rink's ice surface, but there was one individual that, to me, definitely stood out from the others with his constant effort to assure that the boys had a good ice surface to play on. Mr. Bob Culmar was steadfast in his commitment to this cause, and I was eager to meet with him on any given night when he would be able to flood the rink. Mr. Culmar had access to some high-capacity water pumps from the company he worked for. This effort was quite something to me. You see, Mr. Culmar didn't have a son, but then again, I'm sure his daughter Donna also made good use of the rink.

The four teams' Managers have selected players from the boys wishing to play hockey this year. I ended up on a team coached by my dad and Mr. Moger.

The positive news; Serge, Gilles, Dickie, Donald, Howie, and I are on the same team this year. Now for the unbelievable, shockingly 'Bad' news, we would be wearing the uniform of the Toronto Maple Leafs. We all thought that this had to be a joke.

Living in the heartland of the Montréal Canadians, Les Canadiens, the Habs, nothing could be more shameful than ever having to wear a Leaf's sweater.

How was I ever to walk into my bedroom again. With pictures of the Rocket, the Boomer, Harvey and Beliveau covering my walls. How was I to ever sleep in my bedroom again?

Boys were crying, wanting to go home and refusing to put this loser's sweater on. I can't remember how they talked us into wearing Toronto's hockey sweaters. More likely, the trauma has been forever buried so deeply in my subconscious that even Freud wouldn't be able to find it.

This dilemma gave me nightmares; I'd wake up screaming and running like the Devil was after me, with the Canadian players chasing me along Ste, Catherine Street, with my Leaf's jersey on, yelling "Traitor."

The coaches somehow convinced us that we were the only ones who could ever bring victory to a Toronto Maple Leaf jersey. And why would we want to do that? I'll never know.

My dad gave me an area in the basement to practice shooting the puck into an empty stack of wooden butter boxes. A big piece of corrugated cardboard was my ice surface. He showed me how to strengthen my forearm and wrists. He placed a full-size newspaper in the palm of my hand and, using that one hand only, I had to crumple it into a ball.

I spent hours making paper balls and destroying butter boxes with equal time for studying schoolwork and practicing in the basement. My grades continued improving, as did my shooting strength and accuracy.

We barely managed to win our first game, but a win is always a win. Mr. Moger held a team meeting during the week using a chalkboard resembling a hockey rink surface, demonstrating what we did well and, more importantly, our shortcomings.

This extra effort by the coaches would lead us to be talking things over amongst ourselves, too. This effort did bring us together, more as a team. We won our second game, then our third and our fourth. We went undefeated for the season.

The playoffs structure was such that the top two teams would have a one-game playoff for the Championship. Although, our league games were on an outdoor hockey rink. We would play the playoffs on the indoor ice surface at the Ste Therese Arena.

There was a great deal of community support; obviously, the expectation was for our team to be victorious. The organization rented the arena for two hours. Teams would play the championship game first, allotting the remaining time for the third and fourth-placed teams.

At the end of the first period, the game remained scoreless. Their team goaltender was Norman Joy, playing the game of his young life. We knew we were playing well and that things were still going okay.

The second period ended with a little more tension on our bench, with their 1 to 0 lead. We expected that in the third period, Norman would start to tire with our constant assault. Then incredibly, they scored again, and the arena erupted. Now down 2 to 0, and time running out, a sense of panic shrouded our players' bench. Could our only defeat for the entire year be at hand? The crowd was really into the game now. People often tend to pull for the underdogs in sports, which was undoubtedly the case today.

Sensing the inevitable, our coaches called for a time-out with less than two minutes remaining in the game. They congratulated us for the season past and paid respect to today's opponents. Then clearly made us aware that, "The next two minutes will be carried with you the rest of your lives. So go and do yourselves proud, go out there and win the day."

Serge scored at 18: 32 from his position at the blue line. To say there was an explosion of mixed emotions would be such an epic understatement. With defeat less than 30 seconds away, we were at their end of the rink. I was at center, with Gilles and Donald on the wings. Dickie and Serge were playing defense along their blue line. Donald got the puck back to Serge, who shoots, and the Red Light comes on. He did it; Serge scored again, the tying goal at 19:50. The 'ten seconds' would never be forgotten by anyone there that day, on or off the ice.

There was no scoring in the first overtime period as Norman continued to thwart our every attempt to score. Our goalie Howie has kept us in the game from the start of the first period. His play in the overtime was also outstanding. Then it happened. This experience, soon to be a lifetime memory, occurred. Gilles had the puck going into their corner, saw me heading for the net, flips the puck in the air past their defensemen with perfect timing. I'm alone in front of an open net. The arena erupts again as the celebration begins.

In all the celebration and commotion, Gilles grabs my arm and says: "come on, let's watch our friends play." Because of the overtime we just played, these kids only had twenty minutes left out of the sixty minutes allotted to them. Gilles was that kind of a guy, and all our team ended up watching them play.

The Holy Rosary School was the venue for the Awards Night, with Montréal Canadians star forward Phil Goyette handing out the awards. As the team captain, I received the Championship trophy. I was also the leading scorer during the regular season, winning the league's Leading Scorer Trophy.

A photographer for the local newspaper said she wanted to take a picture of me with my hero. I said okay, and went and found Gilles. She said she meant Phil Goyette, so that was how I ended up with a picture of my hero and Phil Goyette.

I went on to win this year's Baseball Batting Trophy and was the Captain of our baseball team. We finished first at the end of the regular season and again were favored to win the Playoffs.

In late August, on a clear sky warm afternoon, our team, coached by Mr. George Wheeler, would meet coach Joe Murphy's team in the year's final game. The Heights community overwhelmingly supported the season's last game, and it had the makings of a good afternoon's entertainment.

During the second inning with coach Murphy's team in the field, he suddenly walks out onto the field bellowing, "Time Out."

Mr. Murphy had a cannon of a voice, with the clarity a concert tenor would envy. Coach Murphy noticed that every one of his outfielders was looking skyward as a plane passed over the ball field.

"Okay, everyone, look up and watch that plane!" Everybody did as Joe's voice carried that much authority; even the umpire was looking up.

Once the plane had cleared the horizon, Coach Murphy gave the all-clear with, "Let's play ball." It's now in the bottom of the ninth inning, and we are losing by one run. With two men out and the tying run on second base, I find myself up at-bat, an opportunity to be either a hero or a goat.

With the league's philosophy of letting every child play regardless of abilities. Coach Murphy calls "time" and makes a substitution, inserting Eric Savage into the left fielder's position. Eric hadn't caught a fly ball all season, so our team is optimistic about the outcome.

The first pitch thrown was a strike that I swung and missed on. The second pitch, I picked up as soon as it left the pitcher's hand and my swing made perfect contact with the ball soaring skyward to our enviable victory.

For some reason, I stopped running on my way to first base and watched as the ball surrendered to the pull of gravity. Eric was standing there with his eyes closed and his glove aimlessly waving around when "thud" he caught the ball.

Coach Murphy led the way onto the field, picking up Eric as the players from both teams congratulated Eric. We didn't win that day, but we didn't lose either.

I would also have had my enlarged appendix safely removed at a hospital in Montréal. These times were undeniably the best days in my young life.

Dr. Paquin

The clowning around started as we eleven-year-olds got changed in the lower level of the Legion. Our hockey team enjoyed yet another victory; it was a great day.

Outside the front door of the Legion, there was a landing, about ten feet square, with five stairs leading to the ground. When the pushing and jostling started, I went headlong, backward, tumbling over someone kneeling behind me. My memory of this incident ends there.

Some parents took me home, and Dr. François Paquin responded. In my parent's bed, my next recollection is awakening with my teary-eyed sister at the bedside. Mom, Dad and Dr. Paquin were worried, hovering over me. Dr. Paquin soon completed his diagnosis, with me having received a brain concussion. I was to be kept awake for the next twenty-four hours. Further investigation later confirmed the Doctors' suspicion. My hockey season had ended for the season.

The Heights was a small country village, with people accessing two family doctors. Both of whom made house calls.

Our family doctor was Dr. François Paquin. Likewise, Dr. LaRose serviced many more families in the Heights. There were two dentists in Terrebonne at that time. Dr. Moreau, a slightly balding man, had a slight stutter. He would do restoration, as well as fillings. Then there was Dr. Comptois, a colossal man who mostly preferred extractions. Both Dentists terrified me.

Both excelled in generating excruciating pain, often associated with dentistry practices of the day. Insecurity followed me for years to come. I was terrified of experiencing such pain again, avoiding dentists.

Dr. Paquin was a nice person, as well as a fine doctor. He was constantly improving the services offered to his patients. He soon had an x-ray machine installed in his office in Terrebonne.

He stitched me up for one sports-related incident or another on several occasions. I caught pneumonia the following winter. Again Dr. Paquin was summoned.

The treatment for pneumonia, at that time, included a "mustard plaster." It was as disgusting as it sounds, but it worked. Dr. Paquin rubbed me with olive oil where the plaster was to help prevent burning.

My fair skin and red hair were very much concerned with this threat of burning. The remedy was mustard powder, flour and warm water. The paste was spread onto a folded tea towel and placed on me. A wool blanket then covered me to keep the heat contained. Every few minutes, Dr. Paquin would check for redness or skin irritation. The prickly itching continued until the twenty minutes were up.

With the mustard plaster removed, the olive oil was washed off, again preventing the possibility of any skin irritation.

My third memory of Dr. Paquin was one year later, while not even being able to keep water down. The pain in my abdomen was excruciating. Dr. Paquin quickly diagnosed me with acute appendicitis and transported me to Montréal Children's Hospital, where they safely removed my appendix.

If there was a flu going around, or mumps, measles, chickenpox, or even pneumonia, I was sure to catch it. On the other hand, Margaret Ann never came down with anything, zippo, nothing.

So I got everything twice, once for me, once for her. Even when they would vaccinate Margaret Ann for various childhood diseases, her body would reject it.

No vaccination scaring did cause issues when Mom took Margaret Ann to register for her first day of school. A vaccination certificate was required; they would also check for the scaring tissue these vaccinations would leave on your arm.

Mom had the certificate, but Margaret Ann didn't show any vaccination signs. A second and even a third attempt ended with the same results. I think that's the definition of insanity, when you repeat the same action, expecting a different result.

It sounds like a situation my blue-eyed, blond, cute little sister could unwittingly create.

St. Margaret's Sunday School

I was nine years old, walking with my dad on our way to St. Margaret's Church. I was wearing my good shoes, good pants, and a white shirt. Dad headed into the Church while I walked along the path to the Sunday School Hall.

My shirt was white until I picked up that stick in the ditch beside the path. Mrs. Trivet shamed me for soiling my good shirt. But I told her it wouldn't have been there if God hadn't wanted me to pick up that stick.

So, here I am in the Sunday School Hall at St. Margaret's Church, taught by Mrs. Trivet and other mothers of the congregation. At the same time, Reverend Trivet was worshiping with the remaining adult parishioners in the Church. Our lessons would last about 45 minutes. Then we would be ushered into the Church via a secret passageway from the hall. Okay, it wasn't really a secret passageway, but it could have.

I often wondered what they didn't want us to see in that Church during those 45 minutes. I'm thinking about the Sacrificial Lamb, and perhaps that's where the blood came from for Jesus when he took the Cup and Drank the Blood of the New Continent.

I kept looking for bloodstains or the rope they used to tie up the poor little Lamb. And why would we need a new continent? I couldn't wait to be confirmed, and then I'll know all the answers and what happens.

In the summer, Reverend and Mrs. Trivet would arrange for the annual Sunday school picnic. A provincial Greyhound bus would arrive to take us to the beach at Cap-Saint-Jacques, near Lac des Deux-Montagnes. The lunch and treats were prepared and supplied by our parents.

Once we arrived, swimming quickly became the order of the day. What a fantastic beach this was. You could walk out forever, with the water still only coming to your knees. We were young, our energy was boundless, and this was just the place to test our limits.

After lunch, we weren't allowed in the water, for the next hour, because of the possibility of getting stomach cramps, but we could play along the shoreline.

Then the races and games would take place, with prizes handed out to the winners. At least I never had to worry about losing any awards on the bus trip home. Swimming in such a large body of water was a wonderful treat. The sand on the beach wasn't nearly as gratifying as the beaches at home in the Heights. After all, there could only ever be one Terrebonne Heights.

Once we boarded the bus heading home, I remember this song we all sang. "We don't care for all the rest of Canada, all the rest of Canada, all the rest of Canada, and we don't care for all the rest of Canada, we're from Terrebonne Heights, we're from Terrebonne Heights, we're from Terrebonne Heights." All the way home, we would repeat the chorus. It never sounded like the friendliest of songs to me. Oh, but I sang right along.

I recall some more activities that benefited most girls living in the Heights. Mrs. Cotton was one more of the giving adults at this time in our young lives who stepped forward to offer instruction in tap dancing. One boy, Donald, joined amongst a bevy of girls in this troop of tap dancers. My sister Margaret Ann, Donna, Audrey, Kathy, Gail, Linda, Norma, JoAnn and Judy, among others, were to benefit from Mrs. Cotton's Cottonette's.

I remember attending several Mrs. Cotton and the Cottonette's concerts at various venues; the Mascouche Community Club, the Legion, and the Holy Rosary school.

Once more typical, giving from individuals with a unique talent coming forward and offering their services to the youth and the kids from the Heights. All of their actions contributed to our character-building and infinite bonding friendships.

Likewise, the Sunday School would organize sleigh rides in the winter months. A dance would usually follow these sleigh rides. Most years, it would be either Mr. Harvey Robinson with his team and sleigh or Mr. Andy Burton with his team and sleigh. Both were terrific horsemen.

The old horse bells rang, announcing the arrival of the big sleigh covered with straw and more sleigh bells. Some parents would follow in a car, or two, for safety reasons.

Once we all clambered up onto the sleigh, we'd be off travelling through the side and back roads of the Heights, singing and carrying on like we had the world in the palms of our hands. Little did we know that we did have the whole world in the palms of our hands at this very moment. It bears repeating, and we had the whole world in the palms of our hands.

To show my fondness toward a certain girl. I would do what I envisioned any eleven or twelve-year-old boy should be doing. I would throw her hat or scarf off the wagon, into the snow, or herself. This caring act would always be a sign of unquestionable affection for her. I couldn't often hear what they might be saying, but they showed a type of emotion that I didn't quite understand.

After the sleigh ride, there would be a dance, and this is where my 'flirting' would continue. When a breakneck rock and roll song started blaring away, this was my chance to impress her, just how cool and into it I was. I'd be vibrating like someone using an out-of-control Jack Hammer while jumping around, nervously dancing. How could this fail? It always did, and I still had so much more to learn in the realm of charming a member of the fairer sex.

I remember the first time a girl let me walk her home after a sleigh ride. I had this crush on Chrissie, a girl in my class at school. The night of the sleigh ride and dance, I hoped that Chrissie would say yes when I asked if I could walk her home after the dance. I practiced in front of the bathroom mirror from when supper ended until I walked to the Church Hall. I knew precisely just what I was going to say.

Okay, this is it. I asked Chrissie if I could walk her home. I was so surprised when she said yes. As we walked along Garden Road, suddenly, the sky was full of stars, and the trees seemed to be singing.

So, here was my chance; I was as prepared as any Boy Scout could be. But every time I went to speak, it sounded like the Dr. had one of those tongue depressors in my mouth. And, only this funny stammering sounding "Ahhh" would come out. Even so, when we arrived at her home, she said, "Thank you for walking me home, Skipper." Skipper, she said my name; she said it. It was a good name. Life was good.

The Anglican Church organized these events, and like every other event in the Heights, it was open to everyone.

It bears noting at this time that the population of the Heights was about 45% English-speaking Anglican, 45% English-speaking Catholic and 10% French-speaking Catholic. After all, we were all just "Kids from the Heights."

Over the years, the townspeople made various efforts to the Mascouche Municipal Council to recognize Terrebonne Heights as a "Solitude," independent from Mascouche. Opportunities came, and chances went. But never entirely delivered past the finish line.

I just remembered my mom's story about my first "crush."

When I was nine, different moms took a group of us kids for the day in a rotation system.

That day, I came home from playing at Mrs. Hobbs and told my mom that Mrs. Hobbs makes the best peanut butter and jelly sandwiches ever.

"Mom, you have to find out Mrs. Hobbs' secret, Mom. What makes them so good, really Mom, you have to find out. They're better than anyone else's moms. It's hard to explain Mom, but they just do weird things to my tummy, it feels like I'm full of butterflies, lots of butterflies."

Mom asked me, "Was JoAnn playing with you there, too?"

"Of course, Mom, she's the daughter."

"Then, I think I know the secret ingredient."

Lewis King School

Once again, on my way to school, it was one of those bitterly cold mornings. So cold the cream would freeze and rise out of the glass milk bottles left on people's front steps by Mr. Robinson.

The cream would tower over the top of the milk bottle, with that stubby cardboard milk cap sitting on top like a sign. One that I would interpret as "a sign from above, a treat from God."

So I would stop and scoop the frozen cream from on top of the bottle, place the cap back on the bottle, and eat my frozen treat. They said that the Lord worked in mysterious ways, and this had to be one of them. And I was very grateful for what I was about to receive.

That is why I would still not be in the schoolyard when the bell sounded more often than not. Yep, another "late" day report for my dad to sign.

I started attending Lewis King School in 1954 while entering the third grade. My mom was a Roman Catholic; however, with my dad being Anglican, I had to be enrolled in the Protestant School Board system. Mom would provide my polio vaccination certificate and pay the annual twenty-five dollar fee for me to attend Lewis King School.

I liked this school right from the start. I attended a much larger school the year before, in Verdun, a Montréal suburb, where I attended Bannantyne Protestant school. The older boys regularly beat me because my mom was Roman Catholic, and some of my cousins attended Catholic schools. These boys also believed I was one of those Irish Catholics, which didn't go over too well.

Getting to know new kids is always awkward, but then you go on your second day and start to meet new friends. These would become the friends that would last a lifetime. It did take me a while to understand that I didn't have to be afraid when walking home after school. When you're a little kid, you hold a lot of things inside.

This school was neat, and somehow, I knew that this was where I belonged, at this Lewis King School in Terrebonne Heights. Once handed out, the teacher would show us how to wrap our textbooks with brown paper, saving them from wear and tear. Wrapping these books was the only time I ever excelled in class, during my early years, by drawing cartoons on these brown paper covers.

The classrooms were big and airy, well-lit with full-sized windows along the exterior wall. While the interior wall, with its small ventilation windows at the top, was about sixteen feet tall, giving the roof a decent slope to handle the snows of a Québec winter.

If the teacher picked you to open these windows, you would get to use that long pole with the hook on end. The oversized coat and boots lockers were at the rear of the classroom. The wall behind the teacher's desk was all chalkboard, with sizeable hand erasers and the chalk laying on the small shelf at the board's base.

The classroom door was also on the interior sidewall, where it formed a corner with the chalkboard wall. There was a big picture of the Queen and the Canadian Red Ensign flag.

Above the chalkboard was a large pull-down roller unit containing various maps of the world's countries. The only pencil sharpener for the class would be on the wall near the door, beside the light switches, with a wastepaper basket in the corner. There was also a globe on the teacher's desk and another waste paper basket beside the desk.

Big square tiles covered the floor, and a large clock was above the classroom door. The windows were low enough that if the community fire siren sounded in the hotter months, the older boys would jump out and leave to go and fight the fire.

Once the King had died, the morning started with the singing of "God Save the Queen." Followed by the Lord's Prayer, I would add, "and to Mr. Robinson for delivering the milk."

I struggled in school in my early years, although the teachers would tutor me when they had the extra time. Nothing seemed to connect for me. This pent-up frustration had to be released somewhere, somehow.

There was an actual, five-foot-long stuffed alligator in the school's furnace room. I would put it in the coat and boot locker to fall out onto whoever opened the door. The teacher's desk drawer was also a prime target for my pranks.

I would often stand out in the hall, and someone escorted me to the Principal's office. In the third grade, I was there so often that the Principal threatened "That he would have a coat hook put on the wall for me."

I wasn't the only one; Howie often got the strap in front of the class. This time, the teacher tells Howie to hold out his hand as the belt makes contact with his hand. He grabs the strap. The teacher continued trying a few times, getting more irritated, telling him to stop holding the strap. Howie won't let go of the strap the next time, and with the teacher furiously scolding Howie, her false teeth pop out of her mouth. That poor teacher was never the same after that, and I promised never to become a teacher that day.

Two things happened to me in the fourth grade, Mrs. Cheney, the teacher from heaven, and the school had decided to install an ice rink with hockey boards.

Once they had a hockey rink at the school, my visits to the Principal's office and my behavior changed dramatically. Playing hockey became the core of my existence. I did not want to spend one more day in detention after school hours. I would carry my skates and hockey stick to school and play hockey at lunch hour rather than eating. I would drink my chocolate milk first, then put on my skates, hoping that lunch hour would never end.

Hockey, too, was now related to Math. How many goals were scored if Billy scored two goals in the first period and Skipper scored one and a half times that in the third? I started getting B's and the odd A. Okay, there wasn't the odd A, but things were heading in a better direction.

With Christmas came all of the pageants, the room decorating, the Carol singing, and the thought of having no school for ten straight days. I always wished I were Catholic at Christmas because they got two weeks off at Christmas, including the celebration of the Epiphany. Then again, Protestants got more time at Easter to celebrate; I don't know what we got more time off to celebrate, Easter Bonnets, maybe?

With the middle of January arriving, the school would organize a school "toboggan party" down at Chez Hervé in Mascouche. The hills were quite long, well-groomed, and a pile of fun, for sure. The toboggans all fit nicely into the starting shoots at the top of the run. As I recall, this event wasn't only for Lewis King students; by welcoming all.

There were some dug-out starting places where you would place your toboggan at the top of the hill, but it was more like a free-for-all once you travelled a short distance. The run was a relatively smooth one, providing some incredible downhill speeds. Then we would have to drag our toboggans back up the hill for the next run.

Everyone was having a great time, laughing, and screaming as people would get knocked off their feet by a passing toboggan, with all kinds of funny things happening. Just before our next run, Serge told me he brought something with him that was supposed to make a toboggan go super-fast. "Really," I said, "super-fast; why not try it then." So he took out this can and sprayed the bottom of our toboggan.

Right from the start of the run, we knew that there was something different. We shot right through the steeper run at the top of the hill. So quickly was our speed increasing that we were holding on for dear life. Now I knew what they meant by 'grease lightening'. Poor Kenny never knew what hit him as he walked across the bottom of the hill heading for the path leading back to the top of the run. We took the feet out from under him, and the last I saw of him, he was cartwheeling over us and our toboggan.

The toboggan crashed through the bottom barrier, then continued to slash across an old cornfield. Finally, this super-possessed toboggan came to a rest. Looking back, we couldn't even see the hill, and I asked Serge what the hell was in that can. He said something new called WD-40.

Then, in March, a return trip to Chez Hervé was in order during the spring Maple Sap running days. This time for a sugaring off party at 'la Cabane à Sucre'.

It would start with a horse-driven sleigh ride, and then we'd get a tongue depressor to roll up the poured-out maple syrup over the fresh white snow. We'd roll this into these great big gobs of maple candy. Next, the menu was a serving of "fèves au lard," baked beans with pork and maple syrup.

Maple trees would be tapped back in the day, and the sap collected in buckets. A horse-drawn sleigh with a round vat would travel the trails throughout the maple woods. These buckets would be brought to the sleigh and poured into the vat. The sugar shack was usually located on a hillside, allowing the sleigh to draw near the upper level at the rear of the sugar shack, allowing the sap to be gravity fed, to the waiting wood-fired vaporizer, on the story below.

Besides education, the teachers of the day had so many varying roles to play. There wasn't a winter when someone wouldn't get their tongue stuck to one of the solid steel columns at one of the school entrances on a sub-zero day. Once again, a teacher would have to answer the call.

Being assigned to Lewis King School, I'm sure some teachers had a certain presumption of finding less than well-educated students in this remote village. The teachers would quickly rebuff this theory, joining a long list of great educators and teachers who entered Lewis King School's hallowed halls.

Students wishing to further their respective educations elsewhere could, more often than not, meet the entry requirements and prove themselves well.

My friend Vincent once shared some interesting facts about Lewis King School. Regarding how the school came to be. In the late 1940s, Misters Thacker and Temperton were in charge of the new school project for the Heights. They realized an issue with the number of students currently attending class. They were insufficient to meet the required numbers to justify a new school.

Enter Vincent's grandfather, Mr. Fred Robinson, who convinces M. Chayer, that for five dollars, all twelve of his children will be in attendance, at the existing school, on the appointed day.

One must remember that not one of M. Chayer's children could speak a word of English during this charade. Fortunately, once Dr. Lewis King witnessed the overcrowding of the existing school, he agreed that the current school was indeed too small.

Then to seal the deal, so to speak, the committee's application included naming this new school to be Lewis King School, The contract was signed, and construction started on Lewis King School the following year. How easily history could have been different.

Mrs. Cheney

In 1956, I was entering the fourth grade in Lewis King School. My time in grade three had been very frustrating, not only for me but also for my poor dad.

He would spend hours, and we're talking capital "H" hours with me, going over spelling exercises and math problems. I managed to get a passing grade, but it was only that, a passing grade. Dad had spent the last three nights working with me; on the fourth night, I said, "Dad, all work and no play make Johnny a dull boy."

Dad: "A dull boy, this is coming from my son, my son who has his own coat hook in the principal's office…really…a dull boy."

I could still hear Dad muttering as he walked away; "A dull boy, a dull boy…oh, I hope he has a son."

School at this time was a sheer struggle for me and my father, too, I'm sure. Orally, I would spell words correctly, get the times' table right and solve math problems. But, once the time for the test came, I would have to write out my answers. I would often use the correct numbers and letters in the wrong sequence.

Lewis King School had so many qualified teachers over the years. My grade four teacher would be the best teacher I would ever encounter throughout secondary schooling. I refer to Mrs. Cheney, the teacher who cleared the fog, exposing some very different and rewarding potential for me to envisage.

Shortly into the year, she became aware of my issues. I went from sitting at the back of the class to the front. Then the words no ten-year-old boy ever wants to hear: "I'd like you to stay after school."

Now my mind is racing. Did Mrs. Cheney notice Skippy and me making paper airplanes? Maybe it was when I pulled Chrissie's hair, but it was just a little tug. I couldn't think of another reason; I was pretty good today. Oops, maybe when I tooted, but it wasn't loud and hardly smelled.

No, the reason was that Mrs. Cheney had noticed that the answers were usually correct when I responded orally to questions in class. But when written out, I often got the correct letters or numbers, but I would transpose them in the wrong order.

For weeks, Mrs. Cheney would stay after school and help me slowly overcome this problem; I had no idea what, nor ever heard the word "Dyslexia." It sounded like a terrible foreign disease of some kind. My dyslexia issue turned out to be one of a milder form, one that persists with me today to some degree.

Mrs. Cheney opened this new fantastic door for me, one I eagerly entered. One was where I wanted to go to school and craved more instruction. She gave me a chance to explore my limitations. Now I knew why everyone wanted to have Mrs. Cheney as their homeroom teacher. But her influence didn't stop at her classroom door.

Mrs. Cheney's understanding of awakening an unoccupied mind reveals the best in each of us in many aspects of our education.

Mrs. Cheney met with my parents to explain the circumstances of my dyslexia issue and how to combine these oral and written teaching methods to help me overcome this issue. My dad continued to spend hours with me. Working with me nightly, I could see the frustration that once dominated his face was no longer noticeable.

I think back today about two things. First was the number of hours my dad patiently worked with me while not knowing why I could be this dim-witted. The way he never gave up on his son. Secondly, how easily my life could have taken a very different course. If this remarkable woman, this fantastic Mrs. Cheney, cared so much about her students, she dedicated her entire life to learning.

From organizing school trips to Chez Harvé for a tobogganing party, a sugaring-off party to our school's Christmas recitals, and spelling bees. Mrs. Cheney always seemed to be at the helm, leading the way and encouraging participation by example.

I wasn't the exception to Mrs. Cheney's outreach, not by a long shot. Her outreach encompassed the entire school, from the day she first entered Lewis King School until completing her task.

I don't doubt that every student attending Lewis King School has a Mrs. Cheney story that they would love to share.

Mr. Partridge

Inevitably, during the 50s and 60s in the Heights, our parents worked long, hard hours to provide for their respective families. Mr. Partridge would be one such parent.

He first started his delivery services, providing those much-needed commodities with coal in the winter and ice blocks in the warmer months.

Most married couples of the day would consist of a husband, the family bread earner, and a wife, usually referred to as a housewife, for apparent reasons. Her responsibilities often included the fundamental upbringing of their children and the standard household duties. Couples who also ventured into the business world took on many additional roles. Ones that indeed extended their working hours.

In the wee hours of the morning, Mrs. Partridge (Mary) could be found daily, at the Partridge coal storage building, on Brompton Road. Bagging coal for the day ahead, enabling Mr. Partridge (Fred) to make his door-to-door deliveries.

Without question, we addressed all of our elders, make that any adult, as Mr. and Mrs., or Monsieur et Madame, without question. Likewise, we had aunts and uncles, ou tantes et oncles. Again, without question, never address anyone by their given name, morals being a bi-product of our parent's recent war involvements.

Often I would be walking home from school, and although it was in the dead of winter, I'd be trudging along with my winter coat wholly undone. The flaps on my boots would be open, no hat, no gloves, and that's when I'd hear it, "MOORE! Get those boots and coat done up, and where's your hat, you knucklehead? I'll meet you at the store."

Oh man, again. Yep, it would be Mr. Partridge driving his Oil Truck, coming up from behind me, as I walked home along English Road.

And he always did, I'd find him sitting at our kitchen table having tea with my mom, and then he'd let fly at me again, "Well, Moore, will you ever learn?"

I didn't dare ask, "Learn what?"

His son Clifford and I were the same age and bonded when we first met. Clifford had wiry blond curly hair, a good sense of humor and was level-headed. Perhaps because Clifford and I were sons of business families, we tended to display a decisive leadership role compared to the rest of our friends. I definitely wouldn't ever say that Gilles, Serge, Skippy, nor Dickie, were followers; just at this stage in their development, they were usually content to join the fray.

On a rainy spring day, I went to visit Clifford. I loved walking in the rain as it washed away any traces of winter. It was calming to be alone on a sand road, with the rain dancing off my waterproof cap. It gave me this sense of a connection with the unknown, where insights lay, waiting for exposure.

We begged Mr. Partridge to allow us to play upstairs in Clifford's bedroom. He only wanted to relax in his big chair in the front room and read his book. We finally wore him down, "Stay out of the eaves."

Now staying out of the eaves wasn't easy for eleven-year-old boys. We tried but somehow found ourselves running in the eaves while wrestling on the floor. My foot slipped off a floor joist with enough force to break through the ceiling material below. As I struggled to free my foot, I felt a powerful hand grasp it.

"MOORE, is this your foot?"

Me: "No Sir, it's a stranger's."

We were summoned downstairs and shown the damage.

Then there was the day I sat beside Clifford during a math lesson, and I kept bugging him. Finally, he turned to me to tell me to quit it. At this precise moment, I was attempting to prick his elbow with the sharpened point of my compass. So this is what happens when an unstoppable force meets an immovable object. In this case, penetration depth was substantially more profound than anticipated. We also proved another theorem: for every action, there is an equal and opposite reaction.

With Clifford, in agonizing torment, telling me to "F*%k OFF." He was looking at a suspension or possible expulsion, and the teacher dismissed me from class.

After receiving a call from the school advising me of my required attendance at a special meeting scheduled for 7:00 pm with Mr. Gillingham and Mr. Partridge, I called Clifford. That's when Mr. Partridge answered, saying, "Just be at the meeting, Moore."

Clifford and his dad were already in a classroom with Mr. Gillingham while I waited in the hall. The door opens, and a teacher escorts Clifford to another room, and now I'm walking into the shadow of death, and I'm sure feeling the evil.

The question was right to the point, as Mr. Partridge asked me, "What did Clifford say when you stabbed him in the elbow?"

Okay, I know that the answer is not F*%k off.

"We're waiting, Moore."

"You mean when I stabbed him with my compass," as I'm stalling for time to come up with an answer, any answer, but F*%k off.

"YES, when you stabbed him."

He told me to "frig-off."

Fortunately, the one expression that Clifford was always saying was perfect for the moment, echoing Clifford's statement.

From time to time, Clifford and I would sneak his dad's one-ton flatbed truck out for a spin, the one used for delivering ice. This truck rolled effortlessly when empty. So, with his dad always going to bed early, we would push the truck down a slight incline to a distance, assuring it started silently. Then we would be driving around all of the sand roads in the area. We would return from the opposite direction, shut the motor off, and push the truck down the slope back to its rightful position in the yard.

Then one night, knowing that all the girls and guys would be hanging out around my parent's store. We decided to try our "Hand-braking" donut maneuver. While driving at a reasonable speed, you start to turn while yanking on the hand brake.

Sure enough, as we passed the store turning down Maple Road, a crowd was hanging out in front of the store. So the plan was, with Clifford driving, to go to the end of Maple Road. Turn around and drive back. Then just before the intersection of English and Maple Roads, Clifford would yank on the hand brake and make donuts with the truck.

What could go wrong? Well, for one thing, missing to yank the hand brake. I can't remember if the cable broke or Clifford forgot to pull the handbrake; it isn't relevant. The truck went right through the stop sign, crossing English Road, jumping the ditch bordering Mr. Robinson's vacant lot and then mired in his vacant lot.

Besides the fact nobody was injured with our oversight in judgment, the silver lining was my dad was out making deliveries. My mom threatened us with some words that I never realized my mom knew. Reading between the lines, one could easily interpret her motherly advice to get the damn truck home. The old Ice Truck capers had drawn to an end.

Soap Box Derby Incident

During the 50s and 60s, most kids in the Heights joined these associations when becoming of age; the Brownies, Girl Guides, Wolf Cubs and Boy Scouts. These were some of the groups available at the time.

Throughout this period in Scouts Canada, Akela was the Scoutmaster's title. During these years, we had some terrific Scout Leaders, including and among others, Kenny's dad Mr. Ted Snow, Mr. George Wheeler and Mr. Hugh Walker, being our Akela's, at various times.

As Scouts, we practiced so hard while being taught to march because we wanted to be allowed to participate in the Remembrance Day Parade with members of the Royal Canadian Legion, Branch 120. Marching with these men and women who had served Canada during the Second World War was a great honor.

Most summers, we went camping for two weeks at Camp Tamaracouta and in the woodlands around home, experiencing the wilderness in the depth of a forest. Hiking using a compass, the primary points of orientation, and the many fundamental aspects of First Aid were all experienced. Our motto was "always be prepared." There were no Cub, nor Scout meetings, during July and August.

While reading my new "Archie" comic book, I noticed an ad promoting a Soap Box Derby race in California on the back cover. Wow, what a neat summer project for us guys this year.

I wanted to try making a soapbox car and convincing some friends to participate. As usual, in the end, it was my good buddies, Clifford,

Skippy, Gilles, Serge, Kenny, Dickie and I, who decided to build a Soap Box Derby car.

We all had varying attributes to offer to this project. Clifford was a good organizer, a born leader, and a take-charge guy. Kenny was the organization's brains, but this was not a very high bar level looking around the organization. Skippy went along with any suggestion, as long as he still got to be the inaugural driver. Gilles was the daredevil and always willing to do our test runs. While doing his paper route, Serge was our research and development guy, mostly only the search part of the research for possible components. Dickie, although Dickie logged and recorded all of our activities, he was forever returning some of our prized finds to their anonymous donors. I was our idea man, which, in itself, drastically reduced our odds of success.

It took forever to scrounge up the four wheels and axles needed. You wouldn't believe how some people misinterpret the definition of 'useless junk'. Often, we would be hauling away some orphaned boards, and someone would be chasing after us, down the road, for some unknown reason. We were only borrowing all these things, after all. Well, maybe permanently borrowing.

We also needed a steering wheel, some wooden boards, nails, a rope and tools. We had no clue where to begin, even putting all of our collective knowledge together on how to build a Derby car. Other than noticing some pictures in my comic book featuring a Soap Box Derby contest in California, we were without direction.

Regardless we forged ahead. We eventually assembled something vaguely resembling a Soap Box car, with four wheels, none of which were the same size or style. We would have to continue our search for four matching wheels. Serge and I volunteered to take on finding these four matching wheels. Serge while delivering his newspaper, and I would search while making deliveries for my parent's store. However, the steering wheel was still an old paint can lid. We would keep looking.

While making his Gazette deliveries, Serge spotted a baby pram at Mrs. Murphy's. So the following day, he brought along a pair of pliers to straighten the cotter pins that held the wheels in place on their axles. Serge reasoned we were doing her a favor, as he thought she was getting too old to have more children. So, having no baby pram might help her from getting pregnant.

Dickie recorded the construction process used, all of the parts we stole, no borrowed, no, now I remember, that he would only use the word "recycled." He was away ahead of his time. Regardless, all was documented and logged by Dickie.

While making my deliveries on Poplar Road, I noticed two new constructions started. I told Clifford about my find.

Me: "Today, I saw some boards on Poplar Road. They've been there for a really long time."

Clifford: "When did you first see them?"

Me: "Yesterday."

Clifford: "You're right. They've been there a long time."

Our team had put the main body of the car together. However, our poor construction practices and lack of know-how quickly added unnecessary weight, making pushing harder. Each passing day started to look more like success was just a few days away. But with every 'test' run, more things seemed to fall off or break. Nevertheless, there was a reasonable, albeit slim, possibility that the car might hold together for its maiden run, rolling down a hill on a gravel road.

Late on a sunny Friday afternoon was the day for launching the "Terrebonne Heights Bullet." We pushed our car along English Road to Garden Road. Unfortunately, there were no cheering crowds of encouragement along the way, but some people driving by would point and laugh. We took this as a sign of encouragement and continued to Garden Road. The hill on Garden Road seemed more than suitable to test our entry into Soap Box racing.

We had only ever tested our car on a sand road, with good results up to this point. No one ever got hurt, well, not seriously injured. Besides, we would always "Be Prepared" as Scouts. With these final tests completed on a sand road, it was time to move on to more incredible feats and higher aspirations.

While assuming that the gravel on Garden Road would be a little different in some respects, be a little better, more to the point. One should never assume.

Skippy was very anxious for this special day to happen, as he had volunteered to be the driver, soon be a "Memorable occasion." And at that moment, no one knew just how memorable it would be.

Skippy was the tallest amongst us but not as uncoordinated as usual, with most young lanky kids. Skippy had this habit when concentrating on what he wanted to tell you, where his legs would start tapping and vibrating. First, the table would shake, followed shortly by the entire floor if he didn't stop. This trait was a significant asset when we wanted to test a new additional piece added to the Bullet. If Skippy couldn't shake it off when seated in the car, it was a safe bet that it would survive further activity.

We had a two-pole pushing system to give a better initial start at the top of the hill. So with Skippy now seated in the car, four of us manned the pushing poles. So far, things were running smoother than on a Swiss watch.

The start was great. Amazingly, this was the first time we were all in step with each other, with no one tripping and falling. Skippy was in complete control and kept the car running nice and straight. That was until his speed increased. He went from doing great to going about as straightforward as a terrified chicken with a fox chasing it. At this point on the graveled road, while picking up speed, there was a very noticeable difference in the jostling and bouncing of the car.

Once Skippy started screaming, control might be less than expected. We witnessed Skippy holding the paint lid in the air, hitting the next pothole. We watched in disbelief as, ultimately, the car now seemed to have a mind of its own. Chaos is never a good sign, an omen that never ends well.

The car zigged jerkily to the left side of the road, snapped back to the right, then frightfully plunged off the road into the waiting gulley below. Not merely plunging, more like bounding. Yes, more like bounding, from one mound to another mound. Finally, coming to a rest on its side, at least what remained of the car came to a rest. Skippy, on the other hand, bounced a few more times.

Watching that scene play out, I remembered that Dickie suggested he ask his brother Ted about borrowing his football helmet, the one with the face guard. I'll get Dickie to note that in his 'follow-up' report.

Quickly our medical team rushes to the scene. Kenny and I were shoving each other out of the way, trying to be the first at the accident site. We could see blood everywhere and splatter on Skippy's new shirt. Also, wearing a new shirt is only tempting fate to intervene. I'm sure that Dickie would have noted this in his follow-up review.

Arriving at the scene, we found Skippy with a dazed expression and a large gash on his chin. Being the lead of the Emergency Team, I immediately sprang into action, taking command of the situation. Just weeks before, Mr. Wheeler had given us a First Aid course. He started with slings, bandaging, and minor dressing, then advanced to the more severe use and application of a tourniquet.

I opened our First Aid kit, looking for the mercurochrome bottle. First, dabbing some on the bleeding from Skippy's chin, but there was too much blood, and it quickly washed away the mercurochrome. Pouring the mercurochrome pretty much had the same results. That's when Kenny remembered using a tourniquet from our last Scout meeting. You could always count on Kenny in matters like these.

I'm wrapping my belt around the pressure point on Skippy's neck. Mr. Preston is now scrambling down from the road while yelling at us in a panic. He came tumbling down the embankment, bouncing very similar to the way Skippy had. Then he reached the water, where the Terrebonne Heights Bullet had surrendered to gravity. Apparently, there was a safer way to stop this bleeding.

Skippy, our hero, had survived the great Derby Run, returning from Dr. Paquin's with eight stitches and a shiner. I never realized that Skippy knew so many adverbs and adjectives; he paid more attention in school than I realized. He meticulously described the ordeal, in minute detail, for over ten minutes, of what, in real-time, was about a ten-second encounter. It's always hard for me to understand how some people could embellish a simple story.

However, the Terrebonne Heights Bullet suffered a much different outcome with its total demise. Besides, someone ratted us out, and now Mrs. Murphy was pregnant again and wanted her baby pram wheels back, of which we could only return three. With a promise to keep searching the gulley for the elusive missing wheel.

We went back to racing our bikes around the old tennis court that was once the pride and joy of the members of the Mascouche Community Club. One that no longer flourished, as it once had in its heyday, in days long since lapsed. It was now only a memory at best to those who shared its previous glory days. Most of the poles that had supported the tennis court's netting had long since rotted away, with only a few stubborn old guards still standing at attention. For obvious safety reasons, there remained no potential hazards.

We fixed a central point in the court area that we would ride around while chasing each other on our bikes, always trying to be the fastest.

We never realized these simple, non-consuming days, the ones we were now sharing. These days, too, were destined to be extraordinary memories of the "glory days" for us kids from the Heights.

Younger Years with Dickie

When we were only nine or ten, everyone was always a 'best friend' whenever we played together. Dickie was much more like a brother to me. And like brothers, we would often be fighting. We're talking punching the crap out of each other here. Sometimes I would win, and sometimes, I would be in a lot of pain. Like brothers, five minutes later, we would be playing at something. The past was the past, and we had moved on.

Although Dickie was two years younger than me, he was a pretty big guy, extremely athletic, and intelligent. Dickie also possessed this motherly instinct, a coddling tendency that would lead him to apologize continually for us. No matter the cause, or reason, he was always seemingly trying to calm the waters.

Another important characteristic was his obsession with graphs, charts, and numbers. Statistics and being organized were critical factors in Dickie's makeup.

I remember when the Duncan's moved to their next home, on Brompton Road, in 1957. We decided if all of our friends had bicycles that were forever in need of repair. Perhaps we should open a repair shop at his home.

Amazingly his mom was okay with this idea. She was even encouraging us by providing paper, pencils, and pens. Yes, pens with black ink. Dickie was in his "land of glory." He created graphs, flow charts, inventory lists, invoices, and other documents he thought pertinent. We spent day after day doing this, and Dickie constantly called for "a review" of what had occurred the day before.

I don't remember ever repairing any bikes other than our own; Dickie filled in all relevant data when we did. Compiling these documents is when it became clear why Mrs. Duncan was okay with her son's latest venture. Although the paperwork would be impeccable, Dickie would never physically contact any grease or oil. Dickie's forte in life was unmistakable.

So, it was natural to think there would be statistics when we started playing hockey together on an indoor table hockey game. Dickie's hockey game was the version that included all six NHL teams. Where the players were available to be interchanged at will. Although Boston, Chicago, New York and yes, even Toronto was an option, they would never see the surface of Dickie's game.

With Dickie having the home-ice advantage and selecting the Canadiens, I opted for the Red Wings and the great Gordie Howe. Plus, I liked their 'winged' logo. So we listed our team players on Dickie's "Player's Chart." Charts referenced who scored, who assisted, who was penalized, and who was injured. And yes, Dickie typed out a full recap in his "Hockey News Paper."

One day when I went down to play hockey with Dickie. That's another thing about the Heights; everybody went down…down to Partridges…down to Vermette's, though they were in opposite directions. Nobody ever went up the road; it was down the road, down to the beach, down to the Village. The only option seemed to go 'over'…over to the school…over to the ball field…over to the rink; again, people seemed to very seldom ever go 'up'. Yes, there were a few ups; up to Girl Guides from Brownies and Boy Scouts from Cubs.

However, I digress again, sidetracked one more time, surprisingly off on a tangent. Upon entering Dickie's bedroom, I notice these new switch boxes on a night table by his bed.

What is he up to this time? He turns one switch, and his television comes on; another turns his radio off. He continued creating methods so that he could stay in bed. We thought it was because he was lazy; it seemed he knew where the future lay.

As he developed and perfected more control methods, we all knew he would be 'reviewing' these with us.

My parent's commitment to their store severely limited time for vacations or holidays. Fortunately for me, Mrs. Duncan would always include me in any plans she might have made for herself and her two sons, Teddy and Dickie. My parents were always appreciative and saw that I would be able to go with the Duncans' on their vacations.

Teddy and Dickie were two very competitive brothers. This trait would lead us to some immensely comical and heartwarming experiences. From fishing adventures/ misadventures, from brotherly bowling competitions to watching an entire set of golf clubs being flung into the air, seemingly hovering over the water, surrendering to gravity and unceremoniously splashing in the middle of a pond on a golf course. Their adventures were boundless as was their love for each other. Margaret Ann and I never got to know out younger brother, Patrick, as he died an infant.

La Boulangerie

In the Heights, when you said that you were "going down to the village," everyone knew you meant that you were going to Terrebonne. It always felt like Terrebonne was our big brother.

In the mid to late 1600s, mills were built in Terrebonne, founded in 1720. Legend has it that Terrebonne was once a few residences larger than Montréal when Montréal was still referred to as Hochelaga. The Village of Terrebonne was a fascinating place for twelve-year-old boys to venture independently, explore, and experience.

Gilles, Serge, Dickie, and I would often ride our bikes along English Road and head for the Sand Hill. Before descending the hill, we would go into Desjardins Grocery to buy a bottle of milk and some butter. Then we were off, flying down the hill, heading to the village. It was a glorious feeling, the wind in your hair, the complete freedom felt while screaming down the Sand Hill. It felt like I'd soon be airborne and soaring into the unknown, high above reality.

The road after the hill was long and straight. With nothing but open farmer's fields on either side. We'd always wait for each other at the end of Moody Road by the stop sign. Every time we made that bike trip, we went faster than before. Dickie was the only one of us having a speedometer, but I don't think even Dickie kept track of any of that.

We would then turn left toward the central area of the village. Riding along rue Saint-Louis, we would shortly arrive at a small Boulangerie just off rue Saint-Louis. We'd wait for the fresh baguettes to come out of the oven. Le Boulanger would beg us to let it cool down before eating it. "Ça va vous rendre malade les boys."

Sitting on the shop floor immersed in this bakery's aroma would take me back to my Grandma's kitchen. Watching her kneading the dough and placing it in the oven, I knew this aroma would soon fill her kitchen with that mouth-watering aroma of bread baking.

Something is missing with the connection between a twelve-year-old boy's ears and brain. We heard him all right, but once we opened that door to the outside world, one where we could make our own decisions. Let's say the butter melted fast when the bread made contact with it.

We never got sick. Okay, if stomach cramps are considered ailing, maybe a little under the weather sometimes, but it never stopped us from returning again and again.

Sometimes we'd bring our fishing rods and fish by the old Masson dam or head to the train station to wait for a steam engine. The size of these engines seemed to be so monstrous at the time. Yet, this systematic majestic movement to them was a sort of grace. It was hard to comprehend how this could be; then again, we were also at that age when girls appeared on the horizon. And we had no clue as to their thought process. Yes, I know, some things never change, this being one of them. 'No, not the Trains'

We'd lay pennies on the tracks, turning them into quarters. Dickie wouldn't let us put too many pennies down along the rails in case we derailed the train. On the odd occasion, make that an extremely bizarre event, when we might have gone astray, Dickie would go and apologize, saying that we were good boys and we won't do it again. Dickie, just being Dickie I guess.

My mind would wander as we waited for the huffing and puffing of that old Steam Engine to make its appearance. I would imagine what it would be like to be the Engineer in the cab, looking out along the tracks, listening to the clacking clack and pulling the handle of the train whistle as it neared the next crossing. Although the train had to follow along on the tracks, every bend of the railroad would lead to a new adventure.

We'd soon be heading home to the Heights once again. As we rode along old Moody Road, the grade continually increased as we neared the actual hill. It was a reminder that it wouldn't be too long before we walked our bikes up the Sand Hill. When exhausted, this hill would always seem much longer and steeper.

Once we turned onto English Road, heading for home, the sun would usually be close to setting. Its rays were trying to find a way through the boughs of those big old Pine trees. I was often tired and hungry after a full day of adventures, filled with new and exciting experiences. It was always comforting when the "Moore's General Store" sign came into view.

Friday Night Movies

Friday night in the mid-50s would find people in the Heights heading to the Mascouche Community Club hall to watch this week's movies. The building was of a two-story design, forty feet wide and sixty feet long, with supporting pillars every fifteen feet. The projection room was on the second level at the front of the building.

An enclosed entrance area would keep the hall dark whenever late moviegoers entered the front door. The stairway for the second-level projection room was also in this area. My dad was the projectionist for several years. I'm not sure who made the arrangements for acquiring the movie reels themselves.

Mr. Bill Ball would be sitting inside the hall at a table to the left of the door. He would collect the money as you entered. The canteen was just behind Mr. Ball, where you could buy chips, peanuts, and red or black licorice bags. Cokes and other drinks were also available.

The movie screen was at the far end of the hall, with rows of folding chairs filling the remaining area on the right side of the dancehall. Because you could not see the screen from the left side of the hall, this area would be left void of chairs.

The evening would begin with a few cartoons, followed by a Pathé World Newsreels. There was always a half-hour serial Western movie ending with our hero dangling off a cliff or in another dangerous situation, surely to die. Only next week, we'd find him grabbing hold of the only tree root on the face of the mountain. Amazingly, with his hat still on his head. The feature movie would follow after a short 'Intermission'.

Of course, the next day, my friends and I would be re-enacting the final scene, the one with our hero always found in a grave and dire situation. Then, each of us would take turns playing 'Director', relating how we would have our hero save the day, or more often, himself. We never did seem to guess right, but that didn't stop us from playacting the following Saturday morning.

These Friday night evenings were vital to the health and well-being of a small community like the Heights. There was a cinema in Terrebonne, the Figaro; however, travel for an entire family and higher entrance costs inhibited most families.

Most people would arrive early to catch up with friends that weren't neighbors. These simple times also allowed people to get together for a night of cards to exchange thoughts, aspirations, and difficulties.

So Friday night became much more than merely movie night. It was what people focused on when putting up that last wagon of hay in the haymow, stacking the final cord of firewood, weeding the garden, and repairing the roofing shingles. There was always Friday night, once a week, every week, all summer long.

It was kind of neat having my dad as the movie projectionist. It meant that I would probably be there too. It wasn't so great for my cousins or my dad's teenage nieces, more to the point. Dad paid more attention to things going on below than what was happening on the screen.

If he saw something concerning, to him at least, a young fellow would soon be getting a tap on the arm. The second incident would result in a more formal introduction and a suggestion that you might not appreciate the outcome if I should have to come down here a third time. One of my cousins thought she would die an old spinster, as the boys would move a row or two away, even if they felt that they had heard dad's footsteps.

I'd usually be asleep by the middle of the Western and brought to the projection room, where I would sleep in my dad's arms. I'll bet my cousins relaxed once they saw me heading upstairs.

Now was the era when homes and churches were left open, and your neighbor was your neighbor.

You respectfully used the terms:

"Yes Sir…"

"No Ma'am…"

"Mr.…"

"Mrs.…"

We had aunts and uncles, took your hat off in the house, opened doors for women, stood when introduced, and ended the day kneeling by your bed saying the Lord's Prayer.

Your dad tucked you in, and your mom kissed you good night, telling you she loved you. Life was user-friendly; life was good.

Later on in my life, when things would change, with some people saying: "I knew it was too good to last," I'd look back to these days, these much simpler, easy-going days, and sadly think, I didn't know.

The Telephone

Like most homes in the Heights at this time, we had a telephone at the house on Maple Road. Party lines were the standard service of the day.

The phone was a square wooden box secured to the wall, placed about five feet above the floor level, ensuring that the height of the adjustable mouthpiece for the phone would be adequate to match the range of most people at the time. The listening device or receiver you would hold to your ear is attached to this box. A phone cord connected the phone box and receiver. The essential component of these phones was the crank and bell.

Each residence would have its own 'ring' combination; ours was two long rings, followed by one short ring. Mom had a list of their friend's ring combinations on the wall. I can't remember if there was such a phone book then. The other option was to turn the crank to get the operator quickly, and she would assist you with your connection.

The ring pattern didn't matter much, more often than not. People tended to pick up and ask who you wanted. As time went on, private lines were made available and long sought after. I'm assuming that's where the term "Private line" originated. There certainly was no privacy during this period, using a party line.

The store, for obvious reasons, was one of the businesses that required and had a private line, but these lines were few and far between.

Things remained pretty much this way for many years. Then there was a significant advancement in the telephone industry with the coming of the rotary phone. Slowly this technology extended into the country, and rural areas, including the Heights.

More private lines didn't immediately accompany this new system. However, there were no more confusing ring tones. In the Heights, the exchange code was Granite 7, or GR7, which later became 477. You only needed to dial the last four digits to complete your call at this time unless you were calling someone outside of the 477 exchange. Then, you also needed to dial that particular exchange.

Terrebonne was Normandy 6; then, later, it was 666. You had to lift the receiver and listen for a dial tone to place a call. You would often hear someone telling you they were already on the line.

People rightfully despised using the dreaded party lines. When using the party line, my mom told me that she would say, "Did you hear who was pregnant?" And about five people would say, "No, who?" Mom just wanted to hear how many people were on the line. The Heights seemed to be having conference calls and didn't know it.

By the time we were ten, we were making prank calls. I know, very shocking. We would say that we were from Hydro-Québec and wanted to know if their fridge was running.

Reply: "Yes it's running."

We laughed: "Better catch it before it runs away."

Things like this. Or we would phone asking for Ralph.

Reply: "Ralph doesn't live here."

Us: "Okay, tell him I called…"

After repeating this four or five times, we would call one more time.

Us: "This is Ralph, any messages?"

Then we laughed and hung up; we thought that we were a riot, revealing beyond any doubt our innocence was on full display.

There was a payphone in front of the store—a convenient method of making long-distance calls for many people. Of course, being a payphone, we all had to check to see if there might be some forgotten coins in the return receptacle.

More often than not, there wouldn't be any coins. But not for everyone, it seemed. Every second or third time, I would find fifteen or twenty cents, and my friends would say, I was just so lucky. The truth of the matter was that I would already have fifteen cents in the palm of my hand and let them fall into the receptacle; as I banged on the phone casing with my other hand, I waited to hear: "Aw, man…you are always so lucky."

I recall when Mom let me place my phone order from Eaton's catalogue. Eaton's had spring, summer, fall, and winter catalogues. They also issued a "Christmas Wish" catalogue in early November. Margaret Ann and I always had great delight wandering through these pages, gazing at all the possibilities in their colorful glory.

Wanting a Professional baseball glove on sale in the catalogue, one I had the money to pay for, Mom suggested this would be a good time for me to place the order myself. Pretending not to be nervous, I dialed the order desk. Thankfully, I found myself speaking with a perceptive woman who was more than willing to assist me in completing my order. Of course, Mom was standing by if I fainted or something like that.

Then, I waited daily for the blue Eaton truck with its red logo to arrive with my glove. The phone call, it turned out, was to be the easy part. The waiting, however, was exhausting, and after at least a million days, maybe more, the Eaton's truck finally pulled up in front of the store with my brand new baseball glove.

One more phone memory. I'm not saying that my little sister always got her way. But on the day that Margaret Ann asked our dad for her phone, plus her phone number, with a private line, I was starting to get suspicious. A personal line, while so many households attempted to secure this rare phenomenon of a private phone line. Quickly Margaret Ann's dream became a reality.

I know my dad didn't have this kind of influence today. However, our grandmother, his mother, is a different story. Grandma had a summer home encompassing one side of the mountain on Lake Newaygo. The only phone in this area was at the only store near the train bridge that joined the two lakes. In reality, there appeared that there were two phones in the area.

When we would visit with Grandma at the lake, Dad would use the store's phone to call his mom, and a boat would come to get us. Grandma, to me, had some friends in high places.

Perhaps, it was evident. Perhaps, the writing was on the wall for the Heights as we knew it. And yes, perhaps, it was already on the cusp of disappearing. As the development of the telephone advanced, so did so many others simultaneously. As TV started to outweigh the radio, progress would undoubtedly soon see English Road paved, and gravelling the sand roads would quickly follow. In my eyes, the one 'constant' forever would be that regardless of the many roads life might take me; I would always be a kid from the Heights.

Christmas

It's 1954, and I couldn't be much more excited while pulling on my snowsuit. Knowing that we were going to see the Santa Claus Parade in Montréal, then go to Eaton's Toyville.

My little sister is beside herself, not wanting to wear a dress. She finally relented, and we're waiting for the Greyhound Provincial bus, at the bus stop in front of our store, on English Road.

I truly enjoyed taking this bus trip into Montréal, and since Terrebonne Heights was the starting point of this route, I always hoped to get the very front seat. Mom paid the fare, and we were three seats back.

With Margaret Ann and I wanting the window, Mom would let one of us sit there on the way in and the other on the way home. I always chose the window on the way to Montréal. Because in the morning, the cold old bus always had frosted windows that I could draw on using my fingernail.

After wandering through countless small villages, the bus would finally pull into Dorchester and Drummond Streets terminal. Next, we're on a city bus, heading to Ste. Catherine St., and the Santa Claus parade.

I sat on the curb, watching all the floats and marching bands. I could hear the shouts changing. I jumped up as coming into view were the reindeer, bobbing on their massive float. And then, there was Santa, with an enormous bag of toys you could never imagine. All his elves were tossing candy, lots, and lots, of candy.

Then Mom would bring us to Eaton's fifth floor and their Christmas Toyville. The big brass doors of the elevator opened to this wonderland place, where dreams came true and precious memories were made.

I could hear the bell of old Canadian, Pacific, Engine #2851, clanging as I pulled Mom along with me. Getting in line with my ticket, I envied the train engineer sitting in the coal car while working here for Santa.

It cost twenty-five cents for the ride and a surprise gift at the end of the ride. The three cars were pulled with their brightly colored red seats, allowing two kids to share a seat while meandering through a fantasy maze of Christmas reindeer and elves scenes. Many retired CPR railroaders were responsible for this miracle for us kids.

Then, we would visit Santa to get our picture taken. Margaret Ann was now glad; she wore that stupid dress. I never liked sitting on Santa's knee, fearing that he would recognize me and that his Ho-Ho-Ho would turn into No-No-No. I'm in line thinking that maybe, just maybe. Maybe, I shouldn't have told Margaret Ann that I heard her name called out for the bad little girls while listening to Santa's nightly radio broadcast.

When I got up on his knee, he said, "Have you been a good little boy?"

That's when I jumped off.

After being dragged around the store, while my mom and my aunts went shopping, or 'looking', was more like it. They'd look at something, agree that it was nice, then look at four or five more, only to go back and buy the first one. Unfortunately, this was only my first experience in the realm of female shopping.

Finally, we'd head outside, with Eaton's bags full of stuff, heading to the S.S. Kresge's store. Now, this was more like it.

Entering Kresge's long lunch counter, the swivel back chairs, with seats covered in red upholstery and the red and white floor tiles, were such welcoming sights. Everything was so clean and shiny, the friendly waitresses in their white smocks, the impressive long mirror covering the entire length of the back wall facing the counter. After climbing up on my stool, I ordered a piece of cherry pie and a glass of milk.

While waiting for my pie, I told my mom that I knew what I wanted to be when I grew up, "A train engineer."

Mom said I had lots of time to decide what I wanted to be, but I knew it would always be a train engineer.

We were sitting in the terminal waiting for our Greyhound bus to return to the Heights. I listened to the announcer calling out the bus numbers and their destinations. He would announce one village after the other in a long, monotone, drawn-out voice. I thought it would be so neat to have a job like that.

I said: "Mom."

She said, "I know you've decided what you want to be when you grow up."

How did she know?

Our mom was the Queen of Christmas and decorated to prove it. There would be streamers and icicles hanging from everywhere possible.

Dad would bring home a Balsam Fir tree and let it thaw out. Then Mom would have him place it in an old metal bucket, wrapped in shiny paper, full of coal, and water, anchored to the wall for support.

Margaret Ann and I would help decorate the bottom branches and the ones at the back of the tree. We then watched as Mom would do her magic. Every bulb had its traditional place. The lights had these thin tin wavy protector things to stop the bulbs from heating the tree branches. My favorite ones were those long thin glass tubes filled with liquid that would bubble when they heat up. Then Mom would start placing the icicles on the tree branches, one strand at a time. I might have inherited my patience from my mom, but not so much from my dad.

Toward the last week of November, the Christmas cards would start arriving. I asked Mom if it could be my job to go to our mailbox each morning to check to see what had come. Our mailbox would be transposed into something magical at Christmas, possessing this enchanting aura. It was always special to receive an everyday letter, but it was just Christmas at Christmas: "Magical…"

I would open the mailbox door crammed with cards and letters with such boundless expectations. Once Mom opened and read them to Margaret Ann and me, she would hang them all around the house.

Mom would put a thumbtack high up on the wall, in the corner, close to the ceiling. And then drape string to the next tack at the other end of the wall. Soon, there would be draped cards hanging from every conceivable place. Just an array of colorful, inviting Winter scenes, Santa, with so many reading, "Merry Christmas."

We'd receive carolers at home and would go caroling around the village. Traditionally, Christmas would be on full display in the Heights, with fantastic pageantry scenes and tree lighting displays. Going to the Legion's "Santa Party" was the big event in the Heights. The festivity included games, food, drink, and Santa gifts.

Margaret Ann and I would spend hours sharing the Eaton's Christmas Catalog while fantasizing about what Christmas morning could bring. Margaret Ann quickly circled every other item listed for a girl. Even at this young age, she would always shoot for the stars. I only circled one thing, a Lionel Train Set, and I encircled it so often that Mom said I'd soon be right through the page. This toy train set listed in the catalogue was so similar to the one I had recently ridden on at Eaton's Toyville that I just had to have it.

Christmas morning Margaret Ann and I scampered down the stairs and ran into the front room. In all its grandeur, I was so excited to see the train set waiting under our Christmas tree that I thought I was still dreaming. It was so amazing to see my fantasy become a reality.

The Hudson Steam Engine was there with its operating whistle and a smoke mechanism. It was coupled to a coal car, followed by a tanker car, a boxcar and the red caboose at the rear, all sitting on an oval-shaped set of tracks, ready to depart the station on its maiden run. Dad spent the entire morning playing with me; I would come to remember this particular time and place for the remainder of my life.

I'll never forget the odor from the Lionel transformer once it heated up. I would never forget this unique smell; it was unmistakable. Similar to the smell of those cap gun rolls I used in my toy gun. Some odors are just that memorable.

Dad let me wear the Engineer's cap and control the throttle while he was the Brakeman stationed in the red caboose. Once again, I had the best dad a son could imagine.

Traditionally, isn't 'traditionally' such a very encompassing word; it invokes warm inspiration for me. Okay, where was I? Ah yes, traditionally, we would spend Christmas morning at home, opening gifts and having fun with Mom and Dad. After breakfast, we washed and dressed and visited Uncle Arthur and Aunty Sadie's home on Andrew Terrace with our cousins.

The adults, including our older cousins Dorothy and Lillian, sat around the kitchen table having their Christmas turkey dinner with all the trimmings. At the same time, all six kids would be in the boy's bedroom. For today at least, that had been converted into a classically Christmas dining room for us kids.

Traditionally we would see my dad find an empty bedroom to sleep the day away. At the same time, Aunty Sadie would gather the rest of us around the piano, singing while either Mom or Uncle Arthur played and sang our favorite Christmas songs and carols. I don't know if there ever was a 'perfect Christmas', but these were right up there with the best.

The Corn Boil

Living in the Heights and surrounded by farm country, it would be easy to imagine that we would always get together to have a corn boil in the late summers. Music, song and laughter accompanied these social outings.

Families and friends, year after year, would gather to feast on this year's crop. Each year seems to be better than the previous one. Most were memorable for one reason or another…Somebody was tripping over the cornhusks and taking out a picnic table. Maybe one of the men, overindulging in his beer consumption and starting to quote from the Bible, or Uncle Fred would sing 'the Muffin Man' while balancing a full glass of beer on his head.

But the most memorable corn boil ever, in my memory at least, was when we were older and had access to a car. Not that we had a driver's license, just access to a vehicle.

We would never buy any corn, bought corn never tasted like the ones we could pilfer from someone's cornfield. So, as we got older, our corn boils usually happened a little earlier than most others. Before the corn harvest, we'd take our bikes, ride to the nearest cornfield, complete our harvest, then head to the beach to party on.

So, this particular year in 1962, we had been scouting for the ideal corn raiding location. Serge tells us that he has located one of the best fields we've ever seen. So the plan is hatched. Serge will drive us to the location; Clifford, Fred, Gilles, and I will be dropped off a quarter-mile before the field in question. With it still being daylight until seven, we will only execute at seven twenty; best to keep the plan simple.

Dickie requests a review; first, Serge drops us off. He will then drive away and return to pick us up in forty minutes. Serge will flash his high beams twice. So we will know that he is coming before we head out of the ditch, then completing the render-vous with us. We'll load the booty into the trunk with the mission accomplished. And now only requires the execution of the plan.

We all pile into the car with anticipation and the thrill of the hunt; we head out as the girls are getting things ready to boil the corn on our triumphant return. This corn boil will be 'the' corn boil to remember.

As we reached our destination, Serge slowed the car, dimmed the lights, and gave us our final directions to the field. With our old potato bags in hand, we ventured toward the area. The night was as black as the ace of spades, with no moonlight.

The night air was so still, almost to the point of being ominously eerie. Any sound would travel ten miles tonight. As we neared the farmhouse, we started crawling along the ditch and headed into the field. It was darker than black, it was that dark. We stumbled about the corn stocks, gathering corn as quickly as possible.

Every once in a while, an old farm dog would bark, and the old farmer would yell at him to be quiet. I might add that farmers never took too kindly to our invasions, not at all, with shotguns filled with buckshot always at the ready.

Our forty minutes have passed, and with the harvest gathered, it's just a matter of Serge coming to pick us up. An hour passes with no Serge insight. While watching for Serge, the dogs became restless with our movements in and out of the ditch.

"Where the hell is he…" An hour and fifteen minutes, now house lights were starting to come on. We could hear people outdoors now.

"Where the hell is he?"

Okay, maybe it was much more explicit than "Hell." No, there was no maybe; there were some very detailed swearwords, some that even a Newfoundlander would be proud to utter.

Finally, we see a car coming slowly with its lights flashing, I mean, repeatedly flashing. The only place I had ever seen lights flashing more than this was the neon lights along St Catherine Street on a Friday night.

Unbelievably, Serge starts honking the horn like a distress signal from the Titanic. As he nears us, we could hear him yelling out for us. Serge finally saw us and nearly ran us over. Finally, he stopped as we threw the corn into the trunk. We all jumped in, unsure whether to be laughing or planning his death.

Clifford was the first to ask. "Jesus Christ Serge, what was that?"

Unbelievably Serge forgot where he had dropped us off. He had dropped us off at the wrong field in the first place and had been driving up and down roads trying to remember where it was.

Now that none of us had become dog food, we could see the humor in the situation. I had a great laugh about it; after all, we had a trunk full of corn. The unfortunate part was when we arrived back at the party and opened the trunk. Only then did we discover that we had raided a cattle cornfield. Oh well, you can't win them all.

Halloween Through the Years

Halloween was always great fun and one of those occasions where you could let your imagination rule the day, or the night, would be more precise. Around supper hour, young mothers would venture out with their young ghosts and goblins in tow. The younger teenage crowd usually started their Halloween hijinks around 8:00. Later into the evening, the older teens usually became the mischief-makers until late into the night.

When we were young, my sister Margaret Ann and I enjoyed dressing up for Halloween and going door to door with our mom. There was no fear of sinister deeds back in the day. It was all good fun and, yes, the best of treats. I clearly remember an elderly lady, Mrs. Carnes, who lived halfway down Joy Road at the time. She lived almost directly across from the Wyllie's. She also made the best toffee apples. She always kept one of those bright red ones for both my sister and me.

She would greet us at her door, being completely mystified. As to just whom these two trick or treaters might be. But soon, her parrot, whom I affectionately named "Old Cutthroat," would screech out. "That's the kid, that's the kid, give him a cookie." I always carried Mrs. Carnes's groceries into her home, helped my dad make his deliveries, and always wanted to visit Old Cutthroat. Mrs. Carnes never knew what words might come spewing out of that old parrot. On Halloween, I more often than not dressed like an Old Pirate and dreamt of sailing the high seas with Old Cutthroat.

As the years went by, I was old enough to go door to door with my friends. Clifford and I decided that we should do a few 'tricks' and receive treats. With my cousin Lillian and her husband Doug living directly across from our store, we decided that our first 'Halloween caper' should be soaping their windows.

The plan was for each of us to confiscate the ammo needed for this mission. Our daylight reconnaissance assured us that our victims had not yet stored the wooden deck chairs for the winter. This access was crucial because we were yet too short of reaching the subject windows.

The mission was a complete success. That was until the next day when my mom said that we had to go over and wash Lillian's soaped windows.

Why us? I asked.

"Because you both wrote your names on her windows..." We learned a valuable lesson here that a bit of education can get you into trouble.

When we were thirteen, we managed to talk the older guys into letting us hang out with them. So, we were piled into the back of a car, heading to Brompton Road. Keeping the tradition alive, the guys had decided whose 'old outhouse' they would upset this year. The driver dimmed the car lights and turned the motor off as we approached the 'marked' house.

Silently the car was pushed toward the house and backed into the driveway. One of the older guys tied this old thick rope securely to the back bumper of the vehicle. Our mission was to pull the rope around the old outhouse to encase the building, including the door. After a short discussion about what type of knot would be best, we opted for a Granny Knot. The only one that we could remember.

Our adventure was going to be terrific. Serge, Clifford and I worked together until we accomplished the mission. The car was slowly creeping forward as the rope drew taut with the outhouse now tilted slightly forward. With a roar from the engine, the car bolted forward. The rope snapped, and the outhouse now laid prone on its door, followed by a God-awful scream from someone trapped inside the outhouse.

We stood stunned while we watched the car's taillights disappearing from view. It wasn't a Bible Study class, but an array of "Jesus Christ's" was coming out of us and whoever was in that old outhouse. We stood frozen in terror.

The shocked woman of the house came flying out, finding the man now yelling at her, "to turn the damn outhouse over."

"I can't turn this thing over."

"Then go and get a bloody axe."

Next, she has this menacing-looking axe, and with a full overhead swing, the axe head splinters right through the old fragile wooden walls.

His terrified screams matched her every thrust with the axe.

"For Christ's sakes Martha, be careful with that damn axe."

Now chopping the outhouse wall to splinters, this axe was the last thing I remembered seeing. I was sure that the RCMP would be investigating an axe murder on Brompton Road the very next day.

Maybe we should have stayed and helped upright that old outhouse. But the glint in that crazed woman's eyes told us otherwise. She seemed to be enjoying this much more than perhaps she should have.

The three of us are out of there like lightning bolts, Trying to catch up to our thumping hearts. When we finally felt a safe enough distance away, we stood motionless while gasping for air. While waiting for each other to say anything, only silence filled the night air. We continued to walk in silence until Clifford said.

"Maybe we'll just dress up next year."

Robinson's Farm

The summer was ending, and school would be starting next month, another year over. My calendar ran this way differently.

I identified school starting as the beginning of the year. Potato harvesting happened at the beginning of my year, and "Duchess Potato Chips" had a contract with Howie's dad to use their fields to plant and harvest potatoes. Once Duchess had finished their harvest, the Robinson family could gather the remaining smaller potatoes. Mr. Robinson would use these potatoes as feed for the cows.

We would regularly go to the farm to help out with this task. Our usual crew of Skippy, Serge, Clifford, Gilles and I would show up on the day scheduled. We'd head out into the field, with our old burlap potato bags in hand, and start collecting small potatoes. The area was nice and flat, with deep loamy soil, ideal for growing potatoes.

Once we were nearing the end of the gathering, we'd start talking about the anticipated fun ahead. Then Howie would hitch up Blackie to a low flat wagon, and while slowly driving through the field, we would throw our bags of potatoes onto the wagon.

We'd put the load into the storage area in the barn, and then the fun part would begin. Each of us would get a big bag of those small potatoes and start a potato war in the open haymow of the barn. We were only allowed to throw the potatoes at one another. As, even this way, some of them would hurt. A slingshot could cause severe damage or worse.

It would look like a scene from an old "shoot 'em out" cowboy movie. As we darted in and out of cover, looking for the next opportunity to nail someone on the move. The agility of twelve-year-old boys was on full display here, with those potato wars in Robinson's barn. No one ever surrendered, that I can think of; we ran out of potatoes and energy. Mr. Robinson would later open this area for the cows to come in to eat the evidence from our recent potato war.

Mrs. Robinson would call us for supper, usually for a heaping plate of stew and the best homemade bread. With the sun starting to lower in the sky, Mrs. Robinson would send us packing. We would get our bikes and head for home.

It was a long stretch to get to Colley's corner from the farm, with nothing, and I mean nothing, for miles. Other than the Jeffers home, along the way. Once we rounded this ninety-degree corner at Colley's, it was a short ride to Sullivan's hill, where we would be able to coast down the slope.

As we biked up the other side, where we'd pass by Joe the Barbers, heading along English Road toward the two churches. When we reached the intersection of English Road and Garden Road, Clifford would turn right onto Garden Road, and Skippy left, heading for home.

Serge would be the next drop-off as we passed Wood's store. The Lévesque home was on the left of English Road. As we reached Maple Road, our store lay at the corner of English Road and Maple Road, and I'd be home. Gilles would also turn left onto Maple Road, heading home.

We would all be safely home just before the sun faded from view. A bath before heading to bed would soon reveal the well-earned bruises and welts from a day well spent.

Terrebonne Heights "Field Day"

When one thinks about a cottage and cottage country, it usually invokes one or more of the following visions; waterfront property, clear freshwater lakes, slow-flowing rivers, majestic mountains, low rolling hills, high cliffs or deep ravines. Terrebonne Heights had none of these attributes. Then what made it so unique, so enticing? It was the people, always the people of the Heights.

Today, I sit here some seventy years later, knowing that if there were to be a "Terrebonne Heights Reunion," I would do my best to attend that reunion. Even knowing, full well, that the Heights I remember only exists in my memories. Exceptionally, very little of the infrastructure, nor the landmarks, will be there to greet me. Most, if not all, of the businesses have long since perished. Most family homes have either been replaced or remain unrecognizable today. Some roads have new names, and dead ends go on infinitely. The hills and gullies became level terrain. Even the Legion is now only a memory.

The schools and churches no longer serve as such today. And the absurdity, they paradoxically renamed Terrebonne Heights to Mascouche Heights. Then why would I want to attend a reunion in the Heights? Something that only triumphs in my mind, a "tour de force," if you will. The people have always been the draw, and people remain the same wherever they continue their journey today. Once, each of us was a mere "a Kid from the Heights."

The mid-1940s brought on a surge of new citizens with people from all walks of life. Families were moving in to take up permanent residence from varying backgrounds, points of view, expectations, and prosperity. Nobody fits the definition of monetary prosperity in the true sense of the word. But as for every other category of prosperity, well, there was a significant abundance of each.

The people from the Heights pulled hard together, struggled, and enjoyed life together. When it was time to celebrate, there were no people better than those from the Heights to gather around the Flag pole, laugh and honor, and even mourn together. If you weren't related to somebody in the Heights when you came, there was a good chance you would be before leaving the Heights.

At the end of summer, late August always brought on the Terrebonne Heights "Field Day." A time of camaraderie and festivities galore, with games, competitions and contests. This community gathering was always a celebration, marking the end of summer and the departure of the summer residents and vacationers. The Mascouche Community Club held this annual event on their grounds.

The new larger MCC building was a treasured possession of the community, and the grounds housed a tennis court and a baseball field in its heyday. There was a summer porch on either side of the main hall that extended the entire length of the building. The main hall area incorporated sixteen-foot-high ceilings and hardwood flooring making it ideal for various community functions. There was a canteen area, a kitchen area, a few extra miscellaneous rooms, and those much appreciated indoor washrooms, all on the lower level. The second story housed the movie projection equipment.

The organizers would gather in the early hours to prepare the competition areas for the various races. An essential asset was the sand that composed the Heights, and water would readily drain, making rainy weather less of an issue. Designated crews would ready the sites for the "tug-of-war" and the "Horseshoe" contest. The food and drink would be stored until needed. Youngsters would assist in helping put up the banners and flags.

By midmorning, families would start arriving, and we kids would be set free to vent some pent-up energy stored in anticipation of the day's events.

The 100 yards dash was always fun to watch. The girls were so fast, probably from so much practice, while running away from the boys. I was a pathetic runner, usually finishing near the back of the pack. My only hope was for one of the leaders to trip and fall while taking out a good portion of the field.

The best 100 yards dash was for the men 40 and over, as most of these men still thought they were 19, and all would take off like a bat out of hell until one of them tripped and then the comedy show would begin with people tumbling and whole heartily laughing. Watching this race, I always felt there might be hope for me.

The 3-legged race was always a popular event, as it was a mixed-gender race for all the various age classes, but the adult race was the best one to watch as a lot of the men would grasp their partner by the waist and lift them off the ground while trying to run with them this way. Most would start well, but their forward momentum would reach an imbalance, and the staggering and stumbling would soon follow, with the lead teams taking out the following racers, and the piling ensued.

An equally comical event was the "wheelbarrow" race. Again, a mixed-gender race with the male being the wheelbarrow and the female being the handler. More often than not, the ground speed of the male and the female would get too far out of sync, and both would be going "arse over kettle" to the roar of the crowd.

A more meaningful event would always be the "tug-of-war." This event had many team formats and options from adult males, adult females, youth males, youth females, and mixed teams. These friendly rivalries would carry over from year to year, invoking camaraderie and cheerfulness among the participants and the onlookers.

However, the best, and by far, hands down, was always the final event of the day, the "Greased Pig" competition, held within the confines of the tennis court. It was restricting the possible escape of the little porker.

The "Greased Pig" event was an adult "woman only" event. I must mention that during the ordinary course of any social activity in the Heights, the women were usually quite aware of their appearance, gaining certain respect and a confident expectation.

Not today, nope, they all came dressed for action and determined to become the victor. The women inside the court, each vying for an advantage before the little greased pig was released and greased it would always be. There was more grease on this little fellow than honey in a Beehive.

The enthusiasm would reach a feverish pitch as spectators jockeyed for a better viewing position. The real show was on with the little greased pig's release.

Sportsmanship was quickly a casualty in this event. Respect was out the window, too, as this free-for-all continued. Most times, I could never be sure if there was more squealing from the little pig or the women themselves.

On one occasion, I remember my mom grabbing hold of the tiny pig, but when she squeezed it, the little thing looked like a piece of toast popping out of a toaster.

As the little pig descended, it was met by screams of laughter as it squirted through legs, and arms, coating the women with grease as they tried for its capture and victory.

The women would pile on top of one another, and the little pig would seem to disappear until escaping their grasp. It would be that kind of eye-watering laughter. The belly laughter that consumes you, everyone would be pointing at the action, yet afraid to wipe their eyes if they missed something.

With the games and competitions closing for another year, everyone helped pack up. Then, they said their goodbyes before starting their walk home, reliving some of the funnier moments of the day. Who knew that these unembellished times would be some of the best times we would ever experience.

Rusty's

Every small village has a hub, and Rusty's was the heart and soul of the Heights during the 50s and 60s. It was located in the center of the village and was a magnet to the area's youth and the older teenagers.

The adults of the Heights had the Canadian Legion Branch 120, and the Mascouche Community Club hall was still a concern at the time. But Rusty's, Rusty's was the only place to be in the Heights; it's where it was happening. The TV series "Happy Day's" had Arnold's Malt Shop; we, on the other hand, had the real McCoy in Rusty's.

My first memory of Rusty's was during the winter months when hockey season was the main focus of all ten and eleven-year-olds playing league hockey. We played hockey on an outdoor rink on the grounds of the Mascouche Community Club. It was a wide-open area, where the bitter winds would blow from the North East, and we would have to contend with its strength and bitterness.

Before the game, we would get dressed in the basement of the Legion hall. Likewise, we would return to the Legion after the game. With your feet in a steel-toed boot, and a steel blade attached to this boot, commonly referred to as "skates." We would return to the Legion on most occasions with severely frozen feet. Our moms and dads would manage to get the blood circulating again eventually. But not before we endured the pain associated with the agonizing thawing process. We used to fill our skates with "black pepper" because there was a lot of heat connected to black pepper. So it was more than reasonable for my eleven-year-old mind to think it should do likewise in my skates. Let's put it this way, at best; it might have disguised some of the foot odor often associated with boys' skates and hockey equipment.

Then it was across the way to Rusty's, where we would all scramble through the front door simultaneously, hoping to find an empty stool at the counter. It didn't matter much if you did in the end, as there would be two or three, often more, sharing the stool. We would get a steaming hot mug of cocoa, topped with a big glob of vanilla ice cream that would slowly ooze to a smooth, creamy coating. Once we started to drink this hot chocolate treat, any memory of our frozen feet thawing would be only that, a memory. Life was good for us, "Kids from the Heights."

In the summer months, during this period, Rusty's would be the place to be during the daytime hours for the teenagers of the day. For 25 cents, you would get a hot dog, fries and a coke. You could get a hamburger instead of a hot dog for an additional nickel. That was another thing about the Heights; someone would say they would get a Coke. It only meant that they were thirsty, not necessarily drinking a Coke. It merely indicated that they wanted a soft drink. I never remember hearing the word "Soft drink" ever used.

There were days when we would lull the afternoon away in Rusty's, forming pre-cut cardboard chip boxes for Mr. Blampied (Kenny) during a warm summer's rainy day. We'd talk and laugh while producing a stack of ready-to-use chip boxes. It was a simple task, but it created a good-natured, memorable diversion for my friends and me to pass the day while helping out.

Going through the front door, you would enter the central area of Rusty's. Its long counter is accompanied by large padded stools covered in blue upholstery. The counter also snaked to the left into an add-on section to Rusty's. Directly behind the counters were the business areas of the restaurant. You could place your order while waiting for your meal to be prepared and served, where good times were always happening. There were a few stainless steel milkshake machines along the counter. A milkshake was 25 cents, and there would be at least a glass and a half coming from one stainless steel mixing beaker.

As you walked to the right, you'd enter the dance hall, with its Jukebox and a 'standing' order counter. This dance area would contain various five-cent pinball machines, and there was a ten-cent One-Armed Bandit.

One day, my sister came up to me and asked for a dime to play the one-armed bandit; I told her no, "We're not even supposed to be in here, and I only had a dime anyway." Now my little blue-eyed blonde sister had this way of getting what she wanted.

So, as she pulled the arm of the one-armed bandit, the swirling numbers stopped at the winning combination of 7*7*7, with her winning the jackpot. Wow, the big payout, we were rich. Well, more like she was rich. I, on the other hand, got my dime back. Then she told me, there, now we're even.

With her friends and cute little smile, she's off with a pocket full of dimes. I loved my sister. I was her big brother, after all. And nobody, and I mean nobody, ever messed with my little sister, and I have the scars to prove it.

Some of the younger twenty-year-old guys would still want to sew more of their wild oats in the summer months, still yearning to be unbridled and free. The usual remedy was to purchase a few beat-up old clunkers from old Eddy for ten dollars. These beat-up old cars have undoubtedly seen better days. Most of these cars would have at least one more run in them. We'd watch them pull out of Rusty's, heading down to the Central Hotel or the Happy Home in Terrebonne. In their clunker convoy.

Never being disappointed, we would wait, in the still of the night, where sound travelled until the end of time. Listening, listening while we sat anticipating their eventual calamity, return.

After drinking for a few hours, they would be heading home to Rusty's for the remainder of the evening. On arrival at the hotel, the car with the best brakes now leads on the way home.

Then stops on English Road in front of Rusty's and abandons the car. Each of the following wrecks slammed into the parked "beater" car with little to no brakes. A unique method of parking that was more similar to a "bang-up" demolition derby than an alternative.

With everyone safely back in the Heights and hanging out at Rusty's, old Eddy would come with his tow truck and give the boys two dollars a car. He was hauling them back to his garage to have whatever parts remained usable put back into something resembling a car. To be resold once more, again next Friday, for ten dollars.

Then there was the evening when the older guys sat outside Rusty's, just having a good time and drinking a few beers. Now, Ma Blampied, the "Matron of Law and Order" in Rusty's, would usually tolerate these good old boys' shenanigans, and their beer, as long as they drank it outside.

As the night wore on, the laughter turned into roaring mayhem. Harvey stepped up onto Rusty's side door entrance and started preaching. It wasn't from the Bible, but he was a spellbinding, almost hypnotic orator. One that even a Preacher from the Deep South would envy. Harvey was on fire tonight. I never heard so many, "Thou Art's" and "Blessed Be's" and "in the Name of the Righteousness." Harvey was on a 'staggering' roll, literally.

I would have nothing more to be writing about if things had continued this way, so there remains more to the story.

As the dew settled in for the night, the guy's decided to take their beer inside Rusty's, On most occasions, Ma would look the other way, but they say that each of us has our "line in the sand," the one never to be crossed, without retribution. So, Ma kept telling them to take their beer outside with themselves in hand.

"Get out! The whole bunch of you, Get Out!"

Yvon was the first, "Come on, Ma. It's okay."

"We'll hide it under the counter, Ma."

Then Harvey, Bobby, Jimmy, and everyone there started with, "Come on, Ma, just this one last time."

The tomfoolery and drinking continued, with the boys having a grand old time. Nobody noticed when Ma went back into the kitchen.

But they sure noticed her when she stepped out carrying that big double-barrel shotgun, with her glasses all steamed up. Ma couldn't see that well at the best of the times, but now we were all ducking with her glasses all steamed up.

You never saw six grown men fighting to get out through one seemingly small door, all at the same time. "Tabarnak's" and "Don't shoot, Ma, don't shoot. Please, Ma."

That would be the final time the boys would even think about crossing that proverbial line again, Ma Blampied's line. Considering that Ma's height was only about equal to the length of that shotgun, her control of that big shotgun was chaotic, at best.

There was another popular spot on Joy Road in the Heights, where many older fellows would hang out. Arnold Andrew's Pool Room was direct across from Locas's Grocery and Butcher Shop. There was always the usual activity, as the boys would meet to rack up some balls for a game of pool. The shop was about 20' x 30' and had one billiard table and a small canteen, where an assortment of items was available. We'd often go there to watch the men play pool. Many of them were highly skilled and were lots of fun to watch. The competitiveness would continuously grow as the hours passed, as did the display of these men's creative abilities.

More often than not, someone just seemed to stand out from the rest of the crowd. And in this instance, that person would have been Mr. Cecil Dawe, especially regarding the game of 'skittles'.

Skittles is played on a snooker pool table, using only the white cue ball, a red and a yellow pool ball. There are five "skittles" placed in the center of the table. The black one goes in the middle of the red, yellow, green and brown skittles, each having a different point value. The ball you are playing must make contact with another ball before knocking over any of the skittles to count. Skittles is a very highly skilled game to master.

Cecile was one such master, and he was so calm and steadfast in his approach to the game. He was always setting up his next shot with his current shot. His mannerisms and approach to studying the game gained him much respect in and around this pool room.

The Motorcycle Incident at Rusty's Restaurant

A path from Lewis King School led to Rusty's Restaurant. This path was convenient for people living in the area and kids going to school at Lewis King, starting on Elm Road, at the school's backdoor wandering down a slope, to a gully and running behind, along the opposite side, the Chabot and the Levesque homes. Some old boards lay strewn across the small waterway, connecting with the path, as it continued snaking up the opposite slope, eventually arriving just behind Rusty's.

On a warm Saturday, late afternoon, in September, Gilles, Serge, Dick, Clifford and I trudged along this path, kicking at clumps of earth, splashing things in the water, and punching each other while scrambling up the slope, heading to Rusty's. To our serendipity, we saw three motorcycles as we neared the top of the hill at the side of Rusty's. All seemed to be anxious, anticipating their riders, the way they were mounted on their stands, waiting to go wild. Nothing could be a more incredible and inspiring sight for five thirteen-year-old boys to come across.

As we tried to outdo each other, suggesting who owned these hogs and our knowledge of motorcycles. This one-upmanship led me to overstate that I was a good friend of Harvey Cheney.

Clifford had doubts.

"That's bullshit, man. You don't know Harvey."

As expected, Gilles, Dick and Serge were supplying their confirmation.

"Ya, well, not only do I know Harvey, but he lets me sit on his bike."

Oh, I'm now realizing, shit, man, what have I done.

"If that's not bullshit, get on then…"

Again, there was a trio of harmony gladly providing backup. My mouth is now more than a full minute ahead of what brain cells might be working on in my 13-year-old male brain. My options were quickly fading. So, now I had to tell them I didn't know Harvey. At least, that's what anyone but a thirteen-year-old boy would have done.

As I climbed onto the seat, what could go wrong here? It was one of those "here, hold my beer moments" that I would experience in my later years.

Dick was the first, "Shit, he knows Harvey."

But before anyone could say anything else, me and Harvey's bike were crashing to the ground, trapping my leg. As expected, my four buddies did what buddies do in the circumstances like this. They ran like hell, heading for the ballpark to maybe hide there for a week.

Having managed to free myself, do I run or confess? My young life was flashing before my eyes. For the rest of my life, I would lie in fear of Harvey breaking in my bedroom door and dragging me to my destined demise and into the afterlife.

As I opened the door and walked into Rusty's, booming rock and roll greeted me with roars of laughter, an exuberant party atmosphere. So, now I'm tugging on Harvey's leather jacket, trying to get his attention.

"What do you want?"

As fate would have it, there was suddenly a dead silence in the restaurant as I muttered, "I knocked your bike over…"

I never heard so many gasps as Harvey picked me up by the scruff of my neck and hauled me outside, accompanied by his followers. After assuring me that there was no damage, Harvey asked me.

"Why?"

I told him about my bragging that we were friends. He started the bike and said, "Get on."

My dazed look prompted him to add, "Well if we're friends we should go for a ride and where the hell are your buddies hiding?"

So we were heading for the ballpark and circling the first base, heading for the second, and Harvey said to me, "Maybe you should wave to your friends."

Their gawking stares of disbelief turned to screams of amazement while jumping around like cat's on a hot tin roof.

When Harvey dropped me off at Rusty's, he looked back and asked, "Hey kid, what's your name?"

I replied, "Clifford."

Yvon

This night was going to be depressing as Gilles, and I sat alone on the front steps of Rusty's. It's 7:30 on a Friday night, and there's a good movie showing at the Figaro in Terrebonne. You needed money to get in, and Gilles and I had this issue, with money burning a hole in our pockets.

We earned enough money; it seemed to jump out of our pockets somehow. And no, we weren't feeling sorry for ourselves. We were always like two crows, seeing a shiny object and having to have it. We often would run out of money before we ran out of a week.

Yvon came by looking for a ride to the Hotel in Terrebonne and asked why we weren't with our friends. Yvon gave us each two dollars: "now go, be with your friends."

We weren't anything special to Yvon. Yes, Gilles was his neighbor, and he knew of me, but still not much of a reason to show such kindness. He did it because he could help out where he saw a need.

Over the years, on more than one occasion, Yvon often offered to help us; this was not an isolated incident. Yvon would never allow us to pay back the money he gave us. He was Yvon, after all.

Years later, I drove up to Rusty's in my sports car, a Triumph TR-3. Yvon was looking for a ride to meet up with some friends at the hotel in Terrebonne. I was supposed to be meeting someone myself in thirty minutes at Rusty's. Remembering all the times that Yvon helped Gilles and me out, I drove Yvon to the hotel.

He wasn't his talkative self on the way down; actually, he never said one word since we pulled out of Rusty's. It seemed that he enjoyed how well this car handled at high speeds. The way he was so fixated on the road.

We arrived at the hotel in no time at all. I pulled up in front of the hotel, but Yvon sat there. He was staring ahead, still clutching the passenger's grab bar. His knuckles were this ghostly pasty white shade, his eyes just staring straight ahead.

I went and asked his friends to come out and help. When they saw my car, I heard, "Oh man, Yvon is afraid to drive fast."

In that case, petrified would be an excellent word to describe Yvon. Because there's fast, and then there's getting to the hotel and back, in less than twenty minutes.

Here is an amusing Yvon story that I remember Stan telling me, who was married to my cousin Dorothy. The Wheeler boys, along with Doug, Bobby and Yvon, were walking to the Heights from the Wheeler's farm in Côté George.

It was one of those dark moonless nights with an eerie calmness. Maybe it was because it was close to Halloween, and Mrs. Wheeler had told a few old stories about Grace Church's Cemetery. Spooky would be a good word.

Once they got to Grace Church, they could continue to walk along Chemin Sainte-Marie to English Road or cut the distance in half by going through the Grace Church cemetery and a farmer's field.

Through the cemetery they go, all but Yvon, that is. He hated cemeteries: "evil condemned spirits can reach up from their graves, and pull you underground, by your boots."

"Okay Yvon, we'll meet you at Rusty's, besides, no evil spirit worth his salt, would be out on a night like this." With the boys halfway across the farmer's field.

They heard Yvon, "Wait, wait, I'm coming…don't leave me here."

They could listen to Yvon walking toward them, then running, then the most awful, never-ending, high-pitched scream coming out of Yvon.

"It's got me; it's got me."

Upon reaching Yvon, it became evident that in this blackened shroud of darkness, Yvon had run smack into the broadside of an old cow. One that bellowed out in unison with Yvon.

We should all be lucky to have an older friend like my friend Yvon. A millionaire giving someone in need a thousand dollars is kindness, without any actual cost. An individual giving four dollars, but having ten dollars in their pocket, is beyond humanitarian.

An Oak tree has existed for about nine hundred years. It grows for three hundred years, lives for three hundred years, and dies for three hundred years. Hopefully, at least some of these memories will reflect an old Oak tree and remain in existence in one form or another for nine hundred years.

Old Eddy Ellis

The mornings were usually busy around Old Eddy's Garage every weekday. Most of the breadwinners in the 50s and 60s were men. Most have to travel to Montréal, to their place of work, or business. Most had to travel by car without adequate bus service, sharing rides wherever possible.

The story goes that Mr. Collingwood told Eddie there seemed to be a leak in his car's radiator. Likewise, Mr. King needed his battery replaced. Each man receives a promise of repair from Eddy.

"Okay, just leave your car here on your way home after work, and pick it up the next evening."

Most makes of cars of that era had a lot of interchangeable parts. Eddy would instruct his employees; to take the radiator out of that car, and put it in that car. Take the battery out of that car, and put it in that car. There was a noise in Mr. Wood's transmission. Put more sawdust in that transmission; use the finer sawdust this time.

A few days after Mr. Collingwood picked up his car, with his radiator repaired, his battery died. Eddy replied, "Leave your car tonight, get a lift to town tomorrow and pick your car up tomorrow night."

Eddy always managed to keep most of the cars in the Heights running, at least three out of five days a week, anyway. I'm not sure if any of these stories were true. But one thing is true, that old Eddy was an excellent and good friend.

Another service supplied by Eddy was the snow removal of the roads in the Heights. He hired a lot of men for all of his ventures. Ventures and ventures would be a perfect word to use whenever relating things to Old Eddy.

He was quite a character. With Dad and Eddy being good friends, Eddy had to stop at the store to show Dad his new, well, new to Eddy snowblower.

"This is gonna make me a fortune Sid, a fortune."

And off he went to make his fortune. Dad watched as Eddie started up the old snowblower, then soon heard rocks bouncing off the side of the store. Eddie was heading down Maple Road in a cloud of flying snow and many other flying objects.

Soon the store phone was ringing off the hook continuously. With people from Maple Road describing a scene that could be from a comedy movie, except this one wasn't funny. Home after home, people phoned accounting for the repeated shattering of windows and other damages. Eddy certainly didn't make his fortune, but Dad sold an awful lot of glass when Eddy started blowing snow in Terrebonne Heights.

Another venture for Eddy was to purchase his first school bus. Eddy would buy another within a few years, eventually leading to a good-sized fleet of school buses. Eddy was also awarded a contract to service and maintain the Greyhound Provincial buses. This new contract resulted in constructing a much more oversized service garage.

The roads in the Heights were ploughed and sanded but never salted. So when the Provincial bus stopped in front of our store, on English Road. Giles, Serge and I would hang onto the back bumper of the bus with our skates on. We were hoping to make it to Eddy's. Hanging on was great fun until you hit an area with lots of sand, then we'd look like old pieces of tumbleweed in a Western movie, somersaulting through town.

Eddy would always supply a bus and driver to take our hockey team on road trips. Between the school team and the Terrebonne Heights Eskimos hockey team, a team coached by Bob Wood and Michael Brisebois. We owed Eddy a lot. A debt never paid, as it was a forgivable one.

When Eddy saw us hanging around his garage one day, he asked why we weren't at the rink playing hockey.

"Because we have to share time with free-skaters and other hockey teams."

Eddy called my dad a few days later, "Tell Skipper I had a rink built for the boys to use behind my garage."

It wasn't a full-sized hockey rink, it only had small boards, but it did have lights. It was indeed a Godsend for us. The kindness of Eddy was evident everywhere in the Heights.

Eddy was also involved in local politics, often running to be the Councilor for the Heights. My dad routinely campaigned alongside Old Eddy, supporting his efforts.

My fond memory of Eddy today is a man with three-day beard growth, a cigarette constantly in his mouth. He was talking, coughing and hacking, still with the cigarette in his mouth, while nodding his head in agreement.

One of Terrebonne Heights's many unsung heroes early on was Old Eddy and many people like him. They were the ones who carved out this place, this place we called home.

They weren't legends, perhaps more like folk heroes. People like Old Eddy, Joe the Barber, Jimmy Robinson, Fred Partridge, Harry Joy, Art Kennel, Ma Blampied, Mrs. Cheney, Bobby Leuty, Harvey Cheney; The list goes on, with many other people mentioned in these memories of the Heights. These were some of the characters that gave the Heights its "Character."

We who followed owe them for laying the framework. The framework that we, too, built on during our days in the Heights. Why else would our thoughts be yet returning to the Heights, where we grew up.

Progress having an insatiable appetite, so easily consumed environments like that of Terrebonne Heights. A place that just faded away one day. Yet we continued to contact so many others for untold decades. One might contemplate, "Why?" It has always been the people for me; it has always been the people?

I mentioned playing for the Terrebonne Heights Eskimos, a hockey team in the Heights. I recall designing the crest for that team. Bob Wood arranged hockey games against the boys who were studying for their priesthood while attending the academy at the Manoir Seigneurial de Mascouche.

They always had a good hockey team. These future Priests also hated to be defeated. On more than one occasion, if they were losing after the second period. We would notice that some of their players grew taller between the periods and often sported a three-day growth of beard. Moments like this indeed were a 'miracle' on ice.

Another time, while waiting to board the bus for the trip home after a game at the Manoir, I talked with one of my teammates, Jean-Pierre Chayer. Just about things in general, he mentioned that he was from a family of 16 kids. I said 16. Then he said that he was the last child born.

Now, that honestly astonished me. Knowing how common and often, boys in French Canadian families were named Jean-Pierre. I suggested that his dad, M. Chayer, had taken a real chance while waiting for his last child to be born, hoping for a son, resulting in him finally being able to name a son, Jean-Pierre.

"No, no, Dad already had given the name 'Jean-Pierre', to two, of my nine brothers. But he would forget, and would name another one."

I said this must get confusing at family meals and such. He clarified things for me. Most of his siblings had left home and were already married before he was born. And many of them already had kids of their own.

Jean-Pierre grew up in a household with seven or eight siblings; the rest were already out on their own. Amazing to me, as I only had my younger sister, Margaret Ann. No wonder I loved her so much.

Mr. Thorne's Light Bulb

Another nice thing about spending my adolescence growing up in the Heights was the camaraderie shared among the boys. Not that there was only one group; no, there were many different groups to participate with, with varying interests, with so many guys willing to take on a leadership role.

But before this period, when we were 11 or 12 years old, we would have our own "gangs." I was hanging around with Serge, Clifford, Dickie and Gilles, and we were as thick as thieves. Always protecting each other's backs. And yes, this would constantly be tested, as we always pushed the envelope with curiosity and what-ifs.

In the late summer of '57, I remember us four walking along English Road as nightfall quickly approached. While walking past the Thorne household, Mr. Thorne came out, upset, claiming that we were stealing his front porch light bulbs. I was glad that Dickie wasn't with us tonight because he, without question, would have been apologizing for something we didn't do up until this point anyway. We weren't stealing his light bulbs; the thought had never occurred to us, at least, not until Mr. Thorne made this accusation.

This lightbulb certainly sounded like a challenge, one we were accepting. So, from time to time for the remainder of the summer months and into the early fall, we would dare one another to sneak up to Mr. Thorne's front porch and loosen the light bulb. Now, we weren't sure if others were stealing his bulbs and us loosening the bulbs. However, after loosening this light bulb again, we lay hidden and waited to see his reaction. Getting caught in the act wouldn't go over so well.

As fate would have it, we had some other boys wanting to join our gang. Word of our misdeeds and exploits spread amongst the hormone-energized male youth of the Heights after holding our club meeting in the phone booth in front of my parents' store. We decided to allow one guy to join if, and only if, he passed the initiation test.

Yep, sneak up to Mr. Thorne's front porch and loosen that poor old light bulb without getting caught. We were aware that Mr. Thorne was in 'high' Red Alert mode and stood guard nightly.

Clifford Thacker wanted to become a gang member, and we decided he would be the first to try the initiation test. So, with nightfall approaching, we lie at bay for the 'light bulb' to glow. Clifford knew his mission and seemed well psyched for his assignment. The objective target came on, and I could feel my heart rate increasing as I saw Mr. Thorne's silhouette through one of the side windows, with what suspiciously looked like an axe in his hand. At least to my overactive 12-year-old male mind, it appeared to be an axe. Clifford T. was receiving his final instructions from Clifford and Gilles. The mission was now a 'go'.

It was a night with tension in the air, usually a bad omen. Clifford T. started sneaking down the hill to the side of the Thorne home. We watched as he inched toward the front porch when suddenly, he ducked for cover; shit, so much for my clean underwear; fortunately, it was a false alarm on both counts.

Now that Clifford T. has reached the objective porch, the light bulb is in the ideal range, and Clifford made his move. Whoa, he accidentally removes the light bulb, and with the bulb in hand, the front door comes flying open, with Mr. Thorne breathing fire, frothing at the mouth, and, I'm sure, an axe in hand. "Got you, you little bastard!"

As we continue watching the scene, it is not as expected. I never knew that Clifford was this ingenious.

"Mr. Thorne, I caught three boys stealing your light bulb, I took it from them, and I'm just returning it to you."

Now that's quick thinking. Mr. Thorne looks very doubtful until Clifford added, "I cannot tell a lie, it was Moore, Vermette and Partridge."

Oh, he is a little fink bastard. Assuming he knew that he had failed the initiation, he might as well save his hide.

There was one more incident that I remember about Garden Road. Mr. and Mrs. Barnfield also lived along Garden Road. On the opposite side of the gulley, across from the Thorne's place. The Barnfield's home was back, far off the road with an apple tree situated, closer to the house than the road. This apple tree was 'the' apple tree in the Heights, not just any old apple tree.

It was a well-known fact around the neighborhood that the apples produced from this particular tree were very different for some unknown reason. But the fact that we didn't know why they were that good was irrelevant. The reality that we knew that these were that good was very relevant.

Mrs. Barnfield (Bessie) was the "Warden of the Tree." And the warden she was, absolutely possessed, like a demon. She would quickly put the meanest, ugliest, junk-yard dog to shame on any night. The only thing greater than her obsession to protect and harvest these apples for herself was the obsession and desire of just about every other kid in the Heights to steal them.

We heard the stories of how "Old Bessie" was at her wit's end, trying to prevent the loss of her apples to all the hooligans in the Heights. It wasn't just the guys either. These apples were that good and were also an enticement to the girls.

Meaning that these tree invasions' regularity was almost nightly; I suggested we try on a Sunday evening since most kids would be getting ready for school the following day. We opted for my suggestion.

As planned, just as the sun had started setting on the following Sunday, we were lying in wait. Unfortunately, it was not a drab cloudy night. No, it was one of those crisp fall nights where the still night air was as silent as a duck slowly drifting by on the water. As faint as it was, the moonlight had also begun to be a concern. We were starting to have second thoughts about trying when Gilles said it had to be tonight very decisively. Our mission was a 'go'.

We crawled up and along the white picket fence encircling the Barnfield property. We next opened the gate and waited for any sign of being exposed. With nightfall approaching, their house lights had started to come on. Everything looked as usual as we could expect, at least so far.

We could have easily gathered some of the apples that already lay strewn on the ground. There was an abundance already around the base of the tree. But, as everybody knows, the best apples were always on the upper limbs and branches, just out of reach. Our parents and other adults taught this in our developmental stages. When we were young, we reached for something interesting and attractive to our eyes. Every time it would be moved, just out of our reach. The lesson learned was that all the good stuff in life was always, just out of reach, like Bessie's apples.

Gilles volunteered to climb the tree, which suited me, as I had, and still have, this phobia about heights No, not the Heights. Up in the air kind of heights. Gilles was a little shorter than the rest of us, but he was the most agile. Unquestionably the dare-devil and risk-taker.

It happened with Gilles halfway up the tree, tossing apples to Clifford and me. One, very irritated, Bessie Barnfield came whipping out their front door, armed with a shotgun in hand. Spewing threats like they were going out of style, some of which, I'm sure, would make the Devil himself blush. A madwoman, with streaks blazing from her Dragon-like head, sounding identical to a severely scalded cat in the dead of night.

Clifford grabs the bag of apples, and we are streaking out of there, as we were both sure that we heard the cocking of that old shotgun. Hearing Bessie's vivid description of our soon-to-be fate and the sight of her standing in her doorway with that shotgun had embedded the fear of God in Gilles.

For some strange and unknown reason, Gilles started to climb the tree rapidly. Suddenly we witness him leaping from the tree, his arms fully stretched out, embracing some invisible savior, almost looking like he had decided to give the mercy of his soul to God himself.

It turned out that the menacing shotgun was far less terrifying, simply a BB-Gun, not a shotgun. Nevertheless, Gilles said he would be attending church next Sunday to thank God for his intervention.

Nick Debruin

Springtime in the Heights was such an incredible season, as the winter's snows melted, giving way to new beginnings. We realized our youthful energies could be put to good use in and around the Heights while creating adventures. There were fun things and not so much fun things that came along with the spring. As melted snows always revealed what it had hidden all winter. We all seemed to be helping someone or getting involved with a community project.

Nick Debruin was a willowy man in structure who constantly gave his time and energy to many community causes in the Heights. Nick's charismatic nature assured that these efforts would be paramount to St. Margaret's church interests. Nick had two daughters, Anne and Linda, so maybe this was his way of filling that void of not having a son. Whatever, we were the benefactors of his efforts.

When we were 14, if we helped paint the St Margaret's church ceiling above the altar, Nick would let us drive his car, a big Buick Special 88 edition. The church ceiling was low, a vaulted style that sucked up paint like a blotter. This awkward posture gave us a much better appreciation of Michelangelo's undertaking of the Sistine Chapel.

Nick's rule was that two boys drive together, and boys we were. Just like two-year-old pups, full of energy and clueless. So, regarding Nick's format, Serge and I were the two chosen for our driving reward on this particular early summer evening. I got behind the wheel, and Serge was to be the navigator.

Serge was more familiar with these sand roads, which lay after the populated area of Rawlinson Road ended. Serge was a great navigator and was also very competent with pointing out each of the girls he knew and where they lived in this area. As we excitedly fantasized about our potential futures, we easily missed a corner at a relatively high speed. With the car ending up in a swampy area, way off the road, effortlessly cleared the ditch, and we're talking way, way, way off the road.

We snuck back to get Vincent and Eddy's tow truck, as luck would have it. As we drove the wrecker past the church, Nick was outside to stretch his legs a little. With apprehension, Nick climbed into the truck.

As we finally approached the fateful corner, one that I might add had jumped out of nowhere.

Nick said, "I don't see the car."

Serge said, "You're not looking far enough." (Nice one, Serge.)

Nick: "I don't see it near the ditch."

Serge said, "You are still not looking far enough."

Nick questioned, "How far?"

Serge: "Maybe we should go for a walk."

Nick turned about to look back as we approached the car and said, "I don't even see the road. Just how fast were you going?"

I said: "maybe 25."

Nick laughingly added, "He too once owned a speedometer like that."

After retrieving an extra cable, it was only one extra length, but it was a rather long extra length. Finally, We extracted the car from the swampy bog without evident damage. Yes, thick mud, and reeds, do not constitute damage; they're just a warning.

Nick asked who was driving? Yep, Serge was again quick to identify the driver. Nick told me to get behind the wheel and head down to Terrebonne. Unbelievably Nick was not mad, really, not angry. He just wanted to make us responsible for our actions.

Ushering us through this stage of our adolescence would prove to be quite the challenge for Nick in the months to come, one he wholeheartedly embraced.

We were helping Nick at a farm a month later, and they needed something at the hardware store. Nick sent Serge and me. We had to pass along a narrow laneway bound on both sides with fencing. While driving, Serge watched his side and asked how it was looking on my side. I told him that he hadn't missed a fence post yet, and nailed everyone. Yep, we had to put up the farmer's fence again. Nick was a very kind and understanding man who helped shape our characters.

That was the thing about being raised in the Heights; we all seemed to have many moms and dads who had a hand in raising us into molding our respective characters.

Terrebonne Bridge

Coming to the Heights from Montréal, you must cross the Rivière des Mille Îles via the Terrebonne Bridge. The bridge was a two-span, steel construction truss bridge that was narrow and designed for the traffic of this period.

Its narrowness was always a challenge when two provincial buses would meet and have to pass by each other on this old steel bridge. When we would return from a shopping spree with my mom in Montreal, I was always impressed by the bus driver's skills. Every time this occurred, my face would be pressed against the window, watching the bus brushing the bridge's steel girders.

I understood that Les Frères du Saint-Sacrement de Terrebonne had this bridge constructed and owned and operated the affairs of the Terrebonne Bridge. By providing continuous revenue, this toll bridge paid for the expansion of the Le Collège Saint-Sacrement and the entire Parish of Terrebonne.

When you drove up to the bridge from the Terrebonne side of the river, there was a weather shelter and two wooden booths. One on either side of the roadway, where you would be greeted by the Bridge Commissionaire, in his official Commissionaire's hat and coat. He was standing there with his embossed Bridge insignia waist-belt, full of pouches containing change and various bridge tickets available.

The most common was the twenty-five cents for a Red Return trip ticket for a car. One-way tickets were also available, in a different color. There was even a charge of five cents for a bicycle to cross and return. Sometimes we would drive our bikes down to Terrebonne to be able to buy a bridge ticket, only to cross over and then return. We'd have old hockey trading cards attached to the bike frame, and the card would snap against the bike's spokes as the wheels turned. This snapping would be motorizing our bikes, letting our imaginations transport us into a world of fantasy.

During the summer months, vacationers would start returning home from their summer cottages in the Laurentides on Sunday afternoons. Slowly, the traffic would start to back up from the bridge. Through the village of Terrebonne, extending the entire length of Moody Road, past English Road, that leads to the Heights. Then, they continued to back-up past La Plaine onto the village of Saint-Lin, a distance covering nearly 25 miles.

Every weekend, through the summer months, this scenario would play itself out, and to a lesser degree, during ski season. As the village grew and prospered, this revenue source steadily enhanced the village's resources.

Once the winter months returned and the waters of the Mille Îles froze over, the men heading to work in Montreal would start to drive across the ice bypassing the bridge and its charge. Eventually, even the road snow ploughs would clear the snow from the ice road.

Although I never saw a Provincial bus crossing the ice, I did hear so many stories about it happening. If you hear something often enough, you'll believe it, so I think it's true.

I remember watching the men cutting blocks of ice from the frozen waters of the Mille Îles River to be stored until needed for iceboxes in the summer months. Stationing the Terrebonne Police as a deterrent at the base of the bridge was no accident.

This deterrent, and their speed traps, were well known to the residents and the frequent users of the bridge. These speed traps consisted of two weight-sensitive cables that would lay flat on the highway, spanning both lanes. A calibrated distance separated them, so measuring the time it took to activate the first and second sensor indicated the speed you were driving on their monitor. Some of the truck drivers in the area were known to try to hook these speed-trap cables; this would dislodge them from their base.

It was a simpler time, these days of small steel bridges, wandering bus trips through countless serene villages as people would venture to Montréal. As my mom did, and numerous other moms, accompanied by their daughters while looking for that perfect something. A time sadly destined to indeed expire in the name of progress.

The Bowling Alley

Being recognized for its continuing population growth during the 50s, the Heights became a potential area for business opportunities. This explosion, in particular, presented an option in 1960 for the Sullivan brothers, Andy, Ernie and Jimmy. They were one such group that did so by venturing into the bowling business.

The Sullivans situated their Bowling Alley on Phillip and English Road. This new eight-lane center instantly became popular. Previously, there were several groups from the Heights that had bowling teams. Up until now, these groups had to travel elsewhere to bowl. The facility included a modern seated food counter with the usual food fare. The casual bowler could rent bowling shoes for the day or evening. Meanwhile, a good number of the established bowlers had their shoes. The most serious of them also had their bowling balls.

This opportunity was before the days of automated pinsetters, resulting in many pin-boy jobs becoming available in the Heights. Many of us applied and became pin-boys, receiving a schedule of our days and time of employment.

We knew our work position as "in the pit." The area where the lanes ended with a drop-off of about eighteen inches into the pit. Every pin-boy had to manage two side-by-side lanes. We were hopping back and forth between these two lanes. We would always have to be alert while trying to avoid airborne bowling pins and those inevitable errant bowling balls.

Once the bowler threw each ball, we would jump down from our bench above the pit area. After the final ball of each frame, we would pick up all the pins and place them in a rack above the lane. Then roll the balls back on an inclined ball return to the bowler. Then, quickly jump back up onto the bench. We were repeating this process with each frame ending. We would get paid twenty-five cents for ten frames per player.

There were two challenging types of bowling available at the alley. Beginners usually opted for "duck-pins," the smaller pins style, and the palm-sized balls. Those more experienced bowlers often opted for the more demanding "ten-pin" bowling, composed of larger pins and much bigger bowling balls.

These "ten-pin" balls each had hole inserts for two of your fingers and one for your thumb. These holes served two purposes: one, pick up, and two, to maintain control of the ball.

More often than not, the mixed leagues, comprising males and females, opted for the duckpin game. Ten-pin bowling was the dominator in the men's leagues.

Working as a pin-boy was a very physically demanding job that required great reflexes to avoid personal injury. It was more fun to be pinning for a bowling "League" than for a group of casual bowlers.

The etiquette displayed during these league games was sorely lacking in the latter, exposing you to a lot more risk of getting hurt.

Seriously, sometimes people would deliberately set you up for an injury. When this happens, we often misplace one of the pins slightly off its set position, ensuring they would never get a strike.

The mixed leagues were always good ones to be pinning for, as were the women's associations. There were some outstanding women bowlers. Most of the teams were usually well balanced, giving any group, on any given night, the chance to end the evening victoriously.

The best evenings were the ones that featured one of the unsung players having the game of their life, being encouraged by the more skillful players.

This bowling alley was a much-needed facility and asset to this continuing growth and sense of togetherness in the Heights.

Friday night, the "Men's Ten-Pin" league, was the one that I liked the best to work. Although these men were earnest about the game, there was a display of sportsmanship, fairness, and the best, a display of kidding and good-hearted tormenting. Most evenings, players made pretty impressive shots, and the camaraderie would usually be on fine display.

Some men used a lot of finesse in their style, while others opted for brute force, and then there was Mac McEwen.

Mr. McEwen was a giant of a man, with hands the size of a catcher's mitt. I'm sure he could use a ten-pin ball with no finger holes if he wanted to.

The difference between Mac's style, and others, using brute force was the fluidity of Mac's entire style. From his long, effortless arching swing, which was remarkably smooth to the ball noiselessly making contact with the wooden lanes and, simultaneously, travelling like the speed of the wind to its intended target.

Whoever was pinning for Mac would give the rest of the boys a heads up. Mac's ball didn't just make contact with the pins. It detonated an eruption of wooden pins that could cover the entire "pit" area. Often knocking over pins three or four lanes over. The ball would always make this resounding impacting thud into the padded backboard in the pit, the "Mac thud."

Of course, extra tips always come your way if you were lucky enough to be pinning for the winning team. After the Friday night men's league games concluded, there would often be some other games. These extra games are where, at the time, we made the "big" money.

The Figaro

There was a movie theatre in the village of Terrebonne, the Figaro. Although most of the area residents were French-speaking citizens, the Figaro would be playing Hollywood-made, English-speaking movies every Friday and Saturday evening. I couldn't wait to become 14, so I could go to Terrebonne and watch these movies at the Figaro.

Once we were of age, my friends and I would meet at Rusty's to decide if this weekend's movie was one we wanted to see. Going to see a film was always provisional on two possibilities. One that we had enough money, and two, that the weather looked like it would cooperate. We would have to hitchhike the three miles to Terrebonne to see the movie and then hitchhike back home once the show let out.

'Spartacus' was one such movie that was a must-see movie for me. It was staring Kirk Douglas, Jean Simmons and Laurence Olivier. I loved those imposing epic movies with a cast of thousands, and this was to be one of them. Watching most movies would easily transpose me, but an epic like the Spartacus saga, with its pomp and ceremony, spectacular scenes and pageantry, would consume me.

So, around 7:00 pm, we started walking while hitchhiking down to Terrebonne. We were usually lucky to get a lift to the village, especially when the movie was an epic one like the one playing that weekend. Getting someone to stop to give you a ride on the way home to the Heights was always a hit or miss, with varying circumstances. For example, if the movie were what we referred to as a "Girlie Flic," the guys on a date wouldn't want to pick anyone up for fear of breaking the romantic atmosphere.

Once the movie ended, we'd head up the hill of Blvd. des Braves, where it met with rue Saint Lewis, the main street in Terrebonne. We'd turn left onto Saint Lewis, then break up into groups of two or three to better our chances of catching a lift home. Sometimes we would be lucky, and all manage to get a lift home, and other times none of us would find a ride. Whatever the case, we would always wait at the corner of Moody Road so we could all walk along that dark expanse of Moody Road together. We'd usually know who managed to catch a lift, as they would be looking out the car windows and laughing at us.

Westerns were another big attraction for my friends and me. Again, we would always try to make sure we would all be able to see these features by sharing our monies. I remember "the Magnificent Seven," with Yul Bryner, Steve McQueen and Charles Bronson. Again, we would want to arrive as early as possible to ensure we could get good seats. If you didn't make the Friday night movie, you could always try again on Saturday night.

The Figaro itself was a lovely old-style theatre with a marquee entrance. The movies would be dazzlingly featured, all of these flashing white lightbulbs illuminating the entrance area. The woman that ran the theatre would also sell ice cream sandwiches and other things at the back of the theatre during the movies. Nearby the stairway leads downstairs, to where you could find the bathrooms.

As I said, most times, we would manage to get a ride or wait for each other, who weren't so lucky. Once the parade of cars leaving the movie had passed, we'd start to walk along Moody Road, heading for the Heights. If ever we were partway along Moody Road, a car came by while we were walking. This individual would often stop to pick us up, giving us a ride home.

Then there was the night we went to see the movie "Psycho," with Anthony Perkins and Janet Leigh. Psycho was one of those Alfred Hitchcock horror specials. I have to admit that I jumped more than a few times during this movie and that dreadfully grotesque shower scene had my heart beating faster than the rotor blades on an Apache Attack helicopter. This scene embedded itself forever in my memory.

I wasn't looking forward to trying to catch a lift home after this one. I don't think that there was one comfortable person in the entire cinema, and the odds of anyone in their right mind stopping for a hitchhiker after watching this horror show, in particular, weren't good at all, just about as good as, a mouse tripping up an elephant.

As expected, Clifford and I waited for Serge, Gilles, Dickie, and Skippy, at the start of Moody Road, before starting the long walk home to the Heights. It would have to be one of those deathly black nights, too, with those black low-hanging clouds, which are dense enough to blacken themselves out. Even on the best of nights, this section of the highway always had a foreboding presence. There was so much more than an ominous wind blowing that night, like an eerie, intimidating, howling cry, blowing unimpeded across those open farm fields.

I was the first: "It wasn't nearly as scary as everyone said it would be."

Clifford: "Ya, kind of a letdown really."

Serge and Gilles echoed our comments, while Dickie nodded in agreement but stayed mum.

With none of us wanting to let on, we were terrified while watching Psycho. We walked and talked while laughing at the scenes, trying to make light of them. All the while, our hearts were racing. Then the next thing we'd be saying was that they were a little scary. I noticed that our pace had picked up each time we elevated how frightening some of those scenes were. And the more we talked about the movie, the quicker our stride became, until there was no question that we were all running, as fast as we could, knowing that Psycho was after us.

There was no longer a need to hide our fear, as we had long since exposed our genuine anxiety and terror. We kept an even pace, more of a God-fearing stride to our running. Even the Sand Hill didn't pose a problem to our rate, as we effortlessly ran up it. Once we arrived at the top of the hill, the presence of the Heights was in the air. We relaxed more, venting the anxiety. It was almost like we walked through a mythological porthole to the safety of Terrebonne Heights.

My Dad

As with most memories I have shared, living life during the 50s and 60s in the Heights at a very sustainable pace. Most daily matters required co-operation and physical contact, resulting in a more continuous and personal face-to-face existence with each other.

There always seemed to be more time in life back then. So often, people would take the time, make the time, and share the time. It appears that progress has taken time out of life these days. Time, what a precious commodity we once possessed.

On Saturday evening during the winter months, the radio broadcasting of the hockey game at the Montréal Forum began at the start of the game, at 8:00 pm. I would be sitting with my dad on the couch, listening to Danny Gallivan on the radio, with his play-by-play analysis of the hockey game coming from the Forum in Montréal. The televised version of "Hockey Night in Canada" on the CBC Television network only started at 8:30 pm. This delay resulted from Clarence Campbell, the president of the NHL at the time, fearing the availability of televised games would result in fewer people attending these hockey games. The exact opposite occurred.

Being nine years old meant I would be off to bed at 9 pm, only allowing me to watch a half-hour of televised hockey until I shuffled off. I would always be hopeful that they were still playing the first period. Otherwise, the intermission would be filled with Zamboni cleaning the ice surface at the Forum during my half-hour. No matter how I pleaded, I would soon be dragging my hockey stick up to my bedroom, wearing my Montreal Canadians PJs.

Sometimes, my dad's friends would be at our home watching the hockey game with Dad, and they would start teasing me by cheering for the visiting team. They knew I would soon be standing before them, asking my dad to send them home. My mom would buy puzzles featuring Montreal Canadians team players and help me; Okay, I would help her put them together. Then mom would glue backing to these puzzles and place them on my bedroom walls.

My Uncle Arthur also repaired TVs as a second job. He looked like a doctor when making his house calls, arriving with his little black case. This case would contain the testing equipment for the various vacuum tubes used in television at the time. Uncle Arthur also toted specially designed types of suitcases that included the 30 to 40 vacuum tubes necessary for a television.

On Saturday, Dad phoned and asked Uncle Arthur to drop by to take a look and see if he could fix our TV, which was now on the blink. I couldn't believe it, not tonight, because the Canadians were playing Gordie Howe's Detroit Red Wings. The diagnosis was not good. The picture tube was not working. I begged Uncle Arthur to find a way, any way, to get it working. I asked Dad in a panic, "What about the game tonight?"

Dad told me, "it'll be all right," We'll go to Montreal and buy a new TV. I thought I had to have the best dad in the world to do this.

It was a long drive to Montreal in 1955, but I trusted my dad that we would have time to buy the new TV and then drive home in time to see the game. After all, he promised me that I would see the game tonight.

Finally, we parked the car and walked into the TV store, at least I thought it was a TV store. Everybody in this store seemed to be wearing Canadian hockey sweaters. And someone was selling programs, not that I knew what a program was.

I couldn't believe it, not even with my over-active imagination. A friendly usher greeted us and led us to our seats in the Forum, home of my idols, the Canadians. We were now being seated inside an absolute dream come true. Dad picked me up, and I hugged him tightly, tears coming from my eyes, but no words could come out of my mouth. I knew my mind was busy trying to understand what my eyes were seeing. Even my best dreams could never have prepared me for what was unfolding before my eyes as I gawked in disbelief and squeezed my dad.

I don't remember much about the game, except the Habs won, and Dad and I had a hotdog and drink between periods. Dad bought me a game Program too, filled with many pictures of both teams' players.

I fell asleep as soon as we started on the long drive home. I woke as Dad rolled his window down when he stopped to pay the toll at the Terrebonne Bridge. The weather had become a nasty winter's storm, so much so that even the Bridge Commissionaire leaned in and wished Dad a safe trip home.

I stayed quiet while the car's wipers steadily flopped back and forth, fully laden with wet snow. We slowly winded through the snowdrifts covering the streets through Terrebonne. Dad's old Dodge was well suited with its road clearance and weight to slowly but steadily burst through those snowdrifts.

Finally, we made the turn onto Moody Road, heading for the Sand Hill. So often, Dad would let me sit on his lap and steer the car once we headed up old Moody Road, not tonight. The visibility was rapidly decreasing, and I was so glad that my dad was my dad at this very moment. Dad looked at me, gave my head a little rub and smiled: "Once we're up the hill, we'll soon be home."

We only made it about halfway up the hill before we could go forward no more. Dad backed down to the bottom of the incline. Where he got out to put a set of chains on the rear wheels, then he turned the car around and drove up the hill backward. Nobody had a dad like my dad and his love for me.

Epilogue

Terrebonne Heights was indeed not the Garden of Eden. What it was, though, was an ideal place and time for kids of my generation to get an excellent start in life while we developed our characters. Ones molded by our daily experiences, our awareness of ethics and morals, showing remorse when needed and leadership where demanded.

We understood and appreciated the importance of teamwork, the vulnerability exposed to self-doubt and, importantly, how fragile life can be.

There were celebrations, from births to graduations, to marriages, to retirements, and everything in between. Strife, and hardships, failures and mishaps, anxiety and stress, disease and death, all of the above were also acknowledged and shared by those who cared for you and for those you cared.

We would all soon be young teenagers moving forward toward our destiny. Time itself always had a way of separating spawned connections as we evolved more into our individualities in search of tomorrow. Separations were spurred by furthering our educations, settling down while getting married, starting to raise a family, or being transferred out of the province.

All the usual circumstances that arose provided many different paths that included a multitude of forks in the road. Life led all of us to where we find ourselves today.

We may have been scattered far afield during these times of Covid-19. These isolations necessitated by this virus managed to reunite so many of us kids from the Heights.